Canadian Evidence Law in a Nutshell

2nd Edition

R.J. Delisle

THOMSON
™
CARSWELL

Canadian Cataloguing in Publication Data

National Library of Canada Cataloguing in Publication

Delisle, R.J.
    Canadian evidence law in a nutshell / Ronald J. Delisle. — 2nd ed.

Includes index.
First ed. published 1996 under title: Evidence in a nutshell.
ISBN 0-459-24070-6

1. Evidence (Law)—Canada. I. Delisle, R.J. Evidence in a nutshell. II. Title.

KE8440.D437 2002   347.71'06   C2002-905249-1
KF9660.D45 2002

The paper used in this publication meets the minimum requirements of the American National Standard for Information Sciences — Permanence of Paper for Printed Library Materials, ANSI Z39.48-1984.

One Corporate Plaza
2075 Kennedy Road
Scarborough, Ontario
M1T 3V4

Customer Relations
Toronto 1-416-609-3800
Elsewhere in Canada/U.S. 1-800-387-5164
Fax 1-416-298-5094
World Wide Web: http://www.carswell.com
E-mail: orders@carswell.com

To Gloria

Preface to the First Edition

This brief text was initially intended for the use of law students who are beginning their study of the law of evidence and who might benefit from an overall look at this fascinating field. While a good understanding can only be had by a close analysis of the leading cases and the legislation, it is recognized that students can often profit from a look at the forest before and/or after an examination of the trees. Since this was the purpose, the book follows the organization of my coursebook, *Evidence: Principles and Problems*, and hopefully will be considered a useful companion to the same. As the book was being written it was recognized that the book might also be a valuable guide to the experienced practitioner and judge if only as a reminder of some basics that may possibly have been forgotten over time. It is hoped that the book will also be a good, succinct introduction to the subject for the non-lawyer who must frequently wonder what it is that lawyers are about in the courtroom. I have tried to articulate the principles, the common sense, underlying each of the rules so that one might better understand their purpose.

I would like to thank Julia Gulej, Acquisitions Editor at Carswell for encouraging me to write this book, and Kimberly Aiken, Senior Production Editor for her careful editing. I have tried to accurately describe the law as it appeared to be as of May 30, 1996.

R.J. Delisle

Preface

The structure of the book remains the same. The book emphasizes a principled approach to the law of evidence. It's been six years since the first edition and a lot has happened. There have been major Supreme Court rulings on almost every facet of the law of evidence and it is noteworthy how a principled approach has been adopted in each instance. Attention is paid to *Stillman*, the exclusion of illegally obtained evidence, *Handy*, a clear and unanimous opinion on what had been a confusing area surrounding similar fact evidence, *Darrach*, dealing with rape shield laws, *Lifchus*, explaining what instruction is necessary with respect to the requirement of proof beyond a reasonable doubt, *Arcuri*, resolving the controversy over the judge's task on an application for a directed verdict, *D. (D.)*, expressing caution on the use of expert evidence, *Starr*, describing how to mesh existing exceptions to the hearsay rule with the more modern principled approach, *McClure*, *Brown* and *Mills*, dealing with privilege and privacy concerns and finally *Oickle*, a comprehensive statement concerning the law of confessions.

I have tried to state the law as I understand it as of August, 2002. I thank my colleague and friend Don Stuart for making sure that I was kept up-to-date. I thank Rebecca Duncan for encouraging me in the endeavour. It would not otherwise have been done. I thank Christy Pentland for her careful editing.

R.J. Delisle
September 2002

Table of Contents

TABLE OF CASES

1

Basic Concepts

1. Introduction

The rules of evidence that we will be examining in this book are rules which cover court proceedings, civil and criminal. We will be examining the rules as they are applied when insisted on by the parties to the litigation and when the proceedings are taking place in a courtroom. In other forums, the rules are considerably relaxed. And, indeed, even in the courtroom there is a relaxation at times: at the sentencing stage in criminal matters, for example,[1] or in custody matters when the best interests of the child are being considered.[2] There are, of course, a number of administrative tribunals functioning in Canada and each, by its enacting legislation and by general legislation referable to all administrative tribunals, must follow its own procedures. More often than not these tribunals are more liberal with respect to what evidence might be received. Understanding the basic rules applicable to the courts will, however, assist in appreciating the process before other tribunals.

The rules of evidence are largely judge-made but at times we'll see modifications of the rules by statute. The *Canada Evidence Act*[3] governs federal matters and each province has its own *Evidence Act* governing provincial matters. Roughly speaking, what this means is that evidence in criminal matters is governed by the *Canada Evidence Act* and civil matters are governed by, for example, the Ontario or Alberta *Evidence Act*. Other modifications idiosyncratically appear in other pieces of legislation.

2. The Adversary System

A trial, civil or criminal, provides society with the final forum within which a dispute can be settled. Most disputes, civil or criminal, are settled by negotiation between the parties. It is only when they are unable to reach

---

1 See *R. v. Gardiner* (1982), 68 C.C.C. (2d) 477 (S.C.C.).

2 See *Re C.A.S. Metro Toronto and N.H.B.* (1980), 5 A.C.W.S. 66 (Ont. Prov. Ct.).

3 R.S.C. 1985, c. C-5.

a settlement by themselves that they turn to the courts or administrative tribunals for help. Oftentimes the dispute centres around different appreciations of the applicable law. The parties are agreed as to what happened but cannot agree on the legal significance of those facts. The court or administrative tribunal, operating with agreed facts, provides a legal answer. More often, however, the dispute is caused by different interpretations as to what in fact occurred between the parties. When the parties cannot agree on the historical facts they turn to one of our institutions and ask a third party to make a determination so that the matter can be settled and the parties can get on with their lives. The method of fact determination that we in the Anglo-Canadian common law tradition have adopted is called the "adversary method".

The adversary method is distinguished from the inquisitorial method employed in civil law countries by the role of the judge. In the adversary system the judge is relatively passive. She does not herself conduct the inquiry. She does not investigate. She presides over a contest between two parties and judges the merits of two positions which positions are described by witnesses called by the parties. This system has been justified by common law lawyers as promoting the closest approximation to the truth. The diligence of the parties in ferreting out evidence favourable to their side and the vigour with which they attack their opponent's case are seen as better guarantees of approximating the historical truth than giving the problem for resolution to some governmental official whose motivation will rarely be of the same magnitude as the parties. It is also believed that a judge who stays out of and above the fray is better able to objectively determine what in fact occurred than is a judge who descends into the arena and risks having "his vision clouded by the dust of the conflict."[4]

The adversary system has its critics. It is pointed out that the lawyer representing a party, seeking to win the game, will present only the evidence that is favourable to his client's case and not all the evidence that he might have at his disposal and which might shed additional light on the matter. Also, the ability of the adversary system to gain the truth through a contest presupposes some equality between the parties in their resources and when this is lacking the truth may become simply the view of the more powerful.

A major impediment to our search for truth is that the facts to be discovered by our courts are almost always past facts. We discover them largely through the oral testimony of witnesses who profess personal knowledge about what happened. Their supposed knowledge, their beliefs as to what happened, may be tainted by possible defects in their memory processes or their powers of perception. The witness may, in addition, have a motive for falsifying. When a witness speaks, his narration, his description,

---

4 See *Yuill v. Yuill*, [1945] 1 All E.R. 183 at 189 (C.A.).

may not truly reflect what happened. The witness may be remembering imperfectly. He remembers the person as having dark hair although at the time he saw it as red. Or, he thought at the time that the car was black but the light wasn't all that good and he only had a fleeting glance and in fact the car was blue. Or, the witness may be insincere and may want to deliberately mislead the trier of fact. Or, the witness may be communicating imperfectly: he says the car was going fast but for him 50 km is fast. The trier of fact may be misled by the language chosen by the witness to describe the incident. All of these possible imperfections are explored on cross-examination in front of the trier of fact. Cross-examination by the adversary is a process that is peculiar to the common law method of fact-finding. The trier of fact has to guess whether the witness's testimony is an accurate reflection of what occurred. The witness, we've seen, may also be guessing. We cannot be certain as to what actually happened and we accommodate that fact by the device of burdens of proof. We insist that the plaintiff, or the prosecutor, who makes certain allegations and seeks to disturb the *status quo*, must persuade the trier to a certain standard of belief. Short of certainty, but a belief nonetheless. The trier of fact has regard to what the witnesses have had to say, how they said it, how they presented under cross-examination, and arrives at a belief as to the correctness of the witnesses's belief. The trier cannot, like a scientist, engage in the inquisitorial method, or duplicate, as in a laboratory, the historical facts. Facts as found by a trier are then, frequently, guesses upon guesses. This is the best we can do.[5]

While approximating truth may be pre-eminent, the institutions provided by our society need to settle disputes. The resolution needs to be done in an efficient way. The tribunal does not have the luxury of postponing the decision to a later day when more evidence might be available. The parties and society need a resolution of the matter now. The parties and society also need to believe that the matter was settled in a fair way — fair to the parties, fair to the witnesses and fair in the sense that it protected other important societal interests. The law of evidence seeks to accommodate all of these interests which are frequently competing in their claims. The trial judge uses the rules of evidence to ensure efficiency, fairness and the closest possible approximation to the truth. Counsel must do the same. The rules are there to guide in the endeavour to satisfy the various claims. The wise judge, the wise counsel, recognizes that they are but guides and are not to be slavishly and mechanically applied. Compromises must often be made. When the context of a particular case warrants it, the rule must be disregarded. To do this intelligently, the judge and the counsel must not only know the rule, they must understand it. They must appreciate the underlying reason for the rule so that they can decide whether it merits application. The

---

5 See generally Frank, *Courts on Trial* (1949).

goals, truth, efficiency and fairness are pre-eminent. The rules are there to assist in attaining those goals. They must never be allowed to wag the dog!

Our highest courts have increasingly recognized the centrality of judicial discretion in the application of the rules of evidence.[6] Discretion in the application of the rules of procedure is essential to any model of adjudication. Conscious of the policy on which a rule was based, our courts gauge whether that policy is being advanced by application of the rule in the circumstances of their particular case. Our courts articulate the factors that need to be taken into account if the exercise of discretion is to be sound. Counsel, to be effective, must similarly appreciate the underlying policy of any rule of evidence and the factors to be taken into account in deciding whether to apply a rule of evidence if she is to advance intelligent argument in her particular situation and persuade.

3. The Basic Concepts of Relevance, Materiality and Discretion

(a) Materiality

When parties cannot settle a dispute by themselves and decide to resolve it in the courtroom, they delineate in advance what it is that they allege occurred and why that has meaning according to the substantive law. They select that particular slice of life that they wish to litigate; they do not litigate all of history. In a civil suit, the parties exchange pleadings. The plaintiff alleges that certain things occurred and that by the substantive law, of contract, property or negligence, the defendant is obliged to do something. In response to the plaintiff's allegations, the defendant concedes some and disputes others. In a criminal case, the prosecution alleges that the accused committed a certain crime at a certain time and place. The accused may choose to make formal admissions and, in any event, after disclosure and negotiations, by the time the case comes to trial, the prosecution and accused usually understand what it is that separates them. By this process the parties set out in advance what it is that matters between them. These issues that they have identified are known, appropriately enough, as the "material issues".

Suppose the accused is charged with the provincial offence of possession of undersized lobsters. Defence counsel tenders in evidence a witness who will testify that the accused didn't know that there were undersized lobster in his catch. What does the prosecutor say? "The evidence is immaterial". Notice that by objecting that the evidence is immaterial the

---

6 See, *e.g.*, *Morris v. R.* (1983), 36 C.R. (3d) 1; *R. v. Corbett* (1988), 64 C.R. (3d) 1 (S.C.C.); *R. v. Potvin* (1989), 68 C.R. (3d) 193 (S.C.C.); and *R. v. L. (D.O.)*, [1993] 4 S.C.R. 419.

prosecutor is not arguing that the evidence would fail to rationally persuade a trier of fact regarding the accused's state of mind but rather that the accused's state of mind doesn't matter. It's immaterial. Our courts decided, as a matter of substantive law, that there is no *mens rea* requirement for the offence of possession of undersized lobster; the offence was decided to be one of strict liability.[7] The evidence tendered was relevant to the matter sought to be established but what was sought to be established was beside the point; it was immaterial.

It is not uncommon for our courts to reject immaterial evidence as "irrelevant". This looseness of language is understandable as evidence which does not advance our understanding of a material issue might properly be said to be, colloquially, irrelevant. Keeping the concepts separate does, however, yield greater clarity of thought.

(b) Relevance

We regard our present system of fact-finding as a rational system. It's rational at least insofar as we do not engage in the earlier techniques of trial by ordeal or trial by battle. Each of those trials were attempts to call on the Almighty to directly provide us a witness as to who was in the right. Regarding our system as rational we insist that there be a rational connection between the evidence sought to be led and the conclusion that the proponent of the evidence hopes to be drawn therefrom — a rational connection between the evidence tendered and the proposition sought to be established thereby. We exclude from the trier of fact information which affects the senses only. We seek to include only those items which have a legitimate influence on reason. The first determination that must be made concerning any information which is tendered into evidence is whether the information is relevant. If the judge decides the evidence is not relevant it is not admissible. If the evidence is found to be relevant the court will decide whether the law of evidence should operate to exclude this logically probative material.

Relevance exists if there is, logically, probative value within the tendered evidence. The proponent of the evidence must demonstrate that, based on logic and experience, there is a rational connection between the evidence tendered and the proposition sought to be established thereby. Logical relevance is insisted upon. Though the phrase "legal relevance" sometimes finds its way into the jurisprudence that concept has been specifically rejected by our highest court.[8] The only relevance insisted on is logical relevance. There are no degrees of relevance.

---

7 See *R. v. Pierce Fisheries Ltd.,* [1970] 5 C.C.C. 193 (S.C.C.).
8 See *Morris v. R., supra,* note 6 at 11.

To be relevant the information need not render the material issue more probable than not. It is a mistake to confuse relevance with sufficiency. Evidence at a trial comes in piece by piece. The entire case cannot be built all of a sudden. "A brick is not a wall."[9] You build a case brick by brick. Each piece of evidence, each brick, however, needs to have a legitimate influence on reason. The tendered evidence, to be relevant, must make the desired inference more probable than that inference would be if the evidence had not been led.[10]

There is a fundamental and unavoidable problem resident within the requirement that the evidence be relevant. When we ask the question whether the evidence tendered makes the proposition for which it is tendered any more likely than would be the case if the evidence was not introduced, the law of evidence does not furnish an answer. Relevance is not dictated by the law but by common sense and experience. The judge decides, based on his or her common sense and experience, whether the evidence has a legitimate influence on reason. Determinations of relevance will be informed by the judge's culture, gender, background, social origin and age. The pre-eminent question is whether the judge's common sense and experience are in fact common. Does his or her common sense and experience mirror that of the community? Is it common? Is it sensible? There may, in certain cases, be a requirement to inform the court, perhaps through expert evidence, of how the world really operates. The judge's intuition that fact X frequently accompanies fact Y, making X's presence relevant to Y's, may not accord with another's point of view. If this is noted, counsel may need to be provided with an opportunity to persuade the judge that his or her hunch is not correct and deserves to be rethought in light of another's experience.

Evidence is relevant if it has any tendency to make the proposition for which it is tendered more probable than that proposition would be without the evidence. For evidence to have any value there must be a premise, a generalization that one makes, allowing the inference to be made. Evidence that roses were in bloom, when tendered to prove that it was then springtime, has meaning only if we adopt the premise or generalization that roses usually bloom in the spring.[11] The tendency of evidence to prove a proposition, and hence its relevance, depends on the validity of the premise which links the evidence to the proposition. Sometimes the premise will be indisputable, sometimes always true, sometimes often true and sometimes only rarely

---

9   This famous phrase was coined by Professor McCormick: see *McCormick on Evidence*, 4th ed. (St. Paul: West Publishing, 1992) at 339.

10   See *R. v. Watson* (1996), 50 C.R. (4th) 245 (Ont. C.A.), at 257.

11   For this metaphor and the immediate subsequent analysis, I am indebted to Binder & Bergman, *Fact Investigation* (West Publishing, 1991).

true. But a premise there must be. When a proponent states that the evidence she proposes to offer is "clearly" relevant, it is fair to ask the proponent of the evidence to articulate for the court what premise she is relying on. Why is it clear? If she has no response, no premise, the evidence is irrelevant and must be excluded. If she articulates a premise, the opponent can debate with her the validity of the premise. On what experience does the proponent base her premise? Is there contrary experience? Is the premise based on myth? On unfair stereotypical thinking? Is the premise always true? Sometimes? Rarely? These latter parameters do not affect relevance since relevance has a very low threshold, but may affect the probative worth of the evidence which may cause rejection if the probative value is outweighed by other competing considerations. Approaching discussions of relevance in this way may yield a more intelligent discussion than the oftentimes typical exchange of bare conclusory opinions.

In a murder case, the Crown offers evidence that the accused had a motive to kill the victim. The Crown relies on the premise that persons with a motive to kill have a tendency to act on that motive. Since the accused had a motive it is more likely that the accused killed the victim. In this syllogistic reasoning the major premise can be analyzed. Motive is relevant to a material issue but how probative is it? Do persons with a motive frequently implement that motive? Is the premise always true? Usually true? Sometimes? Only rarely?

(c) Direct and Circumstantial Evidence and Relevance

At trial we seek to establish that certain facts occurred in the past. The evidence tendered to support the existence of a particular fact may be classified as either testimonial or circumstantial. With testimonial or direct evidence, the witness describes the material issue. He testifies to having witnessed the making of the contract, the devolution of the estate, the negligence of the driver's conduct, *etc.* The trier of fact is asked to infer from that testimony that the material facts occurred as the witness deposed. If the witness is regarded as credible the inference is forthcoming. With circumstantial evidence the witness professes no direct knowledge of the matter but describes other matters from which it is reasonable to conclude that the matter at issue did in fact occur in a certain way. If the evidence is circumstantial in nature the trier is first asked to infer that the testimonial evidence is reliable and, second, that from the circumstances thereby evidenced it is proper to infer that the material issue occurred.

A witness might testify that she saw the accused stab the victim. Counsel who called that witness wants to persuade the trier of fact that his proposition is to be preferred; that is, that the accused stabbed the victim. The trier listens to the witness, both in examination in chief and on cross and seeks to determine whether her statement is worthy of credit and the prosecution's proposition is to be accepted. The trier of fact asks whether it is right to infer from the witness's statement about the fact that the fact did indeed occur. The trier considers whether the witness is sincere: are there reasons to distrust her, resident in her biases? Was the witness seen as able to adequately perceive: what were the lighting conditions and how good was her eyesight? Is the witness able to accurately recall: what's her memory like with regard to other matters? Inferring from the witness's statement to the proposition to be established, *i.e.*, that the accused stabbed the victim, is a true problem of relevance. Is there a rational connection? Is it reasonable to conclude from this evidence that the proposition sought to be established is true? But no one speaks of the problem in these terms. This sort of problem is normally spoken of as a problem of credibility. We are here dealing with direct evidence; the witness observed directly the material facts.

Suppose the witness testifies that she didn't see the accused stab the victim but she did see the victim emerge from a building bleeding profusely and that moments later she saw the accused emerge with a blood-stained knife in his grasp. Now we are dealing with circumstantial evidence. The witness has described certain circumstances that she has observed. This presents a true problem of relevance. Is the proposition to be established, that the accused stabbed the victim, advanced in a legitimate way by the evidence of seeing the victim bleeding profusely and the accused with a blood-stained knife in his grasp? Is it rational to use this evidence in determining that the accused stabbed the victim?

Notice that in the case of direct evidence there is but one source of error. The person who describes a stabbing that she witnessed might be mistaken or lying. The trier must decide whether the witness is sufficiently credible that he or she can conclude that the stabbing occurred as described. The witness who says she only saw certain circumstances, wounds to the victim's chest and a blood-stained knife in the hand of the accused, may also be mistaken or lying about those circumstances, but also, even if she's accurate in her description, the inference that the prosecutor wants the trier to draw may not be the correct one. That is why we say that circumstantial evidence has two sources of error: the assessment of credibility and the drawing of inferences. This leads some to conclude that circumstantial evidence is weaker than direct, but it would be a mistake to conclude that circumstantial evidence is always less reliable than direct. Frequently it is more reliable. It all depends on the facts of the particular case.

In a murder prosecution, the Crown introduces into evidence letters written by the accused confessing a great love for the victim's wife. The Crown says that these letters provide evidence of a motive in the accused to kill. A Crown witness testifies that she saw the accused stab the victim.

Which piece of evidence is stronger, more persuasive? The letters or the direct eye-witness testimony?

But suppose that during cross-examination of the eye-witness defence counsel is able to bring out that:

1. The opportunity to observe was momentary.
2. The room was dark.
3. The witness's eyesight was poor.
4. The witness had never seen the accused before.

Suppose also that the Crown, in addition to the love letters, leads circumstantial evidence that a knife capable of inflicting the stab wound was found in the accused's possession, that there were bloodstains on the accused's clothes matching the victim's blood-type and that the victim's prized pocket watch was found in the accused's dresser drawer. Which evidence is stronger? The value of the evidence is thus seen not to be dictated by the nature of the evidence. Direct or circumstantial, the evidence will carry the day if the trier is satisfied in the particular case that the evidence is sufficient.

(d) The Meaning of "Prejudicial" in the Law of Evidence

Sometimes you will hear a lawyer argue that a piece of evidence should be excluded because the evidence is prejudicial. This is not a ground of exclusion. Of course the evidence is prejudicial to the opponent's case. That's why the proponent is offering it! If the evidence wasn't prejudicial it wouldn't be relevant to a material issue. There is, however, a power to exclude if the evidence, though relevant, would *unfairly* prejudice the opponent or distort the fact-finding process. If the unfairness of the evidence outweighs its probative value it deserves to be excluded. The unfairness may occur in different ways. The trier of fact may:

1. exaggerate the probative value that the evidence deserves,
2. disregard the real issue in the case, confused as to what the real issues are, or
3. use the evidence for an improper purpose.

Suppose there is a prosecution for murder. The defence is self-defence. The defence tenders evidence that the alleged victim was a person who frequently beat on people. If permitted, the defence will call many witnesses who will testify that they were brutalized by the alleged victim. The defence maintains this evidence is relevant as it tends to show that on the occasion under review the victim, acting in conformity with his character, was the aggressor. There is no rule of evidence banning evidence of character in such a case. But a trial judge might decide, in his particular case, that the probative value of the evidence was outweighed by the possibility of prejudice to the proper outcome of the trial. The judge might decide that a jury, learning of the victim's character, might disregard the strong evidence against the accused theorizing that the world was well-rid of such a despicable person.[12]

(e) Judicial Discretion

Discretion is everywhere in the law of evidence. The trial judge conducts a trial not just to ensure truth but to ensure justice and fairness and to do so in an efficient manner. Though the evidence is determined to be relevant, and there are no degrees of relevance, there may be seen to be degrees of probative value of any piece of tendered evidence. The trial judge might determine that the probative force of the evidence is tenuous in comparison to the competing considerations of confusing the issues, undue consumption of time, unfair surprise to the opposite party or to the witness, or prejudice to the proper outcome of the trial. In such a case, she will exclude the evidence as the competing considerations outweighed the probative value.[13] The Supreme Court of Canada has recently emphasized that in exercising discretion to exclude evidence because of competing considerations the test is different when the evidence is being tendered by the defence. In that situation the test for admissibility of evidence is whether the prejudicial effect of that evidence *substantially* outweighs its probative value.[14]

Draper v. Jacklyn[15] was an action for damages for personal injuries sustained in a motor vehicle accident. Two photographs of the plaintiff's face were admitted into evidence to help illustrate the testimony of a medical witness as to the condition of a scar at a time within five weeks of the accident. The photographs also showed two Kirschner pins, used to hold fractured bones in place, protruding from the plaintiff's face. The Court of Appeal decided the photographs should not have been admitted into evidence as they were inflammatory and could have distorted the minds of the jury as to the amount of damages to be assessed.[16] The Supreme Court reversed. For the Court, it was a matter of probative value versus the possibility of prejudice. The Supreme Court recognized that it was a matter of judicial discretion and that the trial judge was in the better position to determine whether the photographs would inappropriately deflect that par-

---

12 *R. v. Scopelliti* (1981), 63 C.C.C. (2d) 481 (Ont. C.A.).

13 See *Morris, Corbett* and *Potvin* cited in note 6, *supra*, as instances of the Supreme Court of Canada recognizing the need for discretion in the proper application of the rules of evidence.

14 See *R. v. Shearing*, (2002), 2 C.R. (6th) 213 (S.C.C.).

15 (1970), 9 D.L.R. (3d) 264 (S.C.C.).

16 [1968] 2 O.R. 683 (C.A.).

ticular jury from the fact-finding process. According to the Court, an appellate court should be loath to interfere. The Court recognized that this discretion more regularly occurred in criminal cases but recognized its place in civil cases as well.

(f) Multiple Relevance

The same piece of evidence may be relevant to different matters. There may be a rule of evidence that excludes if the evidence is tendered for a certain purpose but the evidence may be received if tendered for another purpose. For example, suppose the accused is charged with fraud. The accused has a criminal record which includes convictions for obtaining money by false pretenses, perjury and sexual assault. Are those convictions relevant to the material issue? First, what is the material issue? The issue is whether or not he deliberately deceived another and thereby obtained a material benefit. Do the previous convictions make the proposition that he committed the fraud under review more probable than that proposition would be without the evidence of the previous convictions? What does your common sense indicate? Suppose the accused takes the witness stand and testifies that he didn't know that his representations were false. Are the previous convictions relevant to the credibility of the accused as a witness? Does your common sense and experience indicate that the accused's previous convictions rationally support the proposition that the accused may be lying when he denies the knowledge necessary to conviction? If the convictions are relevant to credibility they should be received. Suppose I now tell you that there is a rule of evidence, *i.e.*, a rule that excludes relevant evidence, that evidence of the bad character of an accused cannot be led for the purpose of persuading the trier of fact that the accused on the occasion under review acted in conformity with that character and committed the dastardly deed. What should the trial judge do? She might decide to admit for the one purpose, credibility, and exclude for the other, character. In that event she would give a limiting instruction to the jury that they are to use the evidence for only the one purpose. Or she might decide that in her particular case the limiting instruction would be futile, that the jury would use the evidence for the prohibited purpose, that the accused would be unfairly prejudiced, and she might then decide to exclude the evidence altogether.[17]

---

17 See *R. v. Corbett, supra*, note 6, discussed, *infra*, in Chapter 3, *Witnesses, Accused as Witness*.

(g) Conditional Relevance

Evidence at trial comes in piece by piece. The relevance of a single piece of evidence tendered at the beginning of a trial may not be manifest. In such a case, counsel will offer his undertaking that the relevance will later become apparent as other evidence is led. The judge, in her discretion, will admit the evidence conditionally on the later linking up. If the evidence necessary to fulfil the condition is not forthcoming the trier will be instructed to disregard the earlier piece of evidence. In a proper case, there may need to be a mistrial declared.

4. Relevance of Habit

If a person is in the habit of acting in a particular way, that habit may be seen as circumstantial evidence which has relevance to how he acted on the occasion being litigated. It seems to be a rational exercise to conclude that a person would act in conformity with his habit. If the habit is of invariable regularity, the probative worth is high and the evidence deserves receipt. If the habit is less ingrained, the trial judge will have to determine admissibility by assessing its probative worth against the competing considerations of undue consumption of time, confusion of issues and prejudice to the proper outcome of the trial.

If a medical doctor always performs an operation in a particular way it seems sensible that he be able to testify that he performed the operation under review in that way even though he has no present knowledge of how the particular operation being reviewed was performed. While there may be no direct evidence of how the operation was performed — the doctor may not be able to remember the particular operation — there would be circumstantial evidence in the form of invariable habit.[18] If, on the other hand, the doctor can only say that he's generally a careful person and he therefore probably performed the operation in a certain way, the judge may decide that his evidence concerning how the particular operation was performed is less than useful and exclude. The evidence that he's a careful person is relevant but so general in its nature as to be lacking in the necessary probative value when the competing considerations are taken into account.

---

18 See, *e.g.*, *Belknap v. Meakes* (1989), 64 D.L.R. (4th) 452 (B.C. C.A.). In *R. v. Watson* (1996), 50 C.R. (4th) 245 (Ont. C.A.) the accused sought to introduce into evidence that the deceased was in the habit of carrying a weapon. The proposed witness would, if permitted, say that the deceased carried a gun "like a credit card. He never left home without it". The Court of Appeal reversed the accused's conviction on the basis that this evidence of habit was improperly excluded.

5. Relevance of Character

A person's character, as evidenced by his conduct or reputation previous to the event being litigated, may be relevant to a material issue in the case without the necessity of the trier of fact inferring that the person acted in conformity with his previous conduct or reputation on the occasion under review. For example, in a case of assault, a claim of self-defence might be founded on the accused's belief, based on his understanding of the victim's previous conduct or reputation, that the victim had a disposition towards violent behaviour; such a belief, if honestly held, could cause the accused to view the victim's conduct on the occasion under review with apprehension and so cause the accused to strike out at the victim. In a prosecution for sexual assault, the accused may defend on the basis of mistaken belief in consent and may seek to demonstrate the reasonableness of such belief as founded in his understanding of the victim's disposition towards indiscriminate sexual intercourse which in turn was founded on his appreciation of the victim's previous conduct or reputation. The chain of reasoning which the proponent asks the trier of fact to follow in these cases does not involve the necessity of inferring that a person acted in conformity with his or her character. The evidence of character is led only for the purpose of persuading the trier of fact that the accused's belief was genuine. Whether the law should permit an honest belief in consent to operate as a defence to a charge of sexual assault is a matter for the substantive law to resolve and not for the law of evidence. If honest belief is, by the substantive law, a material issue, then evidence of the victim's character is regarded as relevant thereto.

Occasionally, the character of a person is not just relevant to a fact in issue but rather is itself a material issue, an operative fact which dictates rights and liabilities. For example, in an action for defamation in which justification is pleaded, the plaintiff's reputation or character is the determining factor.

The above scenarios present few problems for the law of evidence. The following is not concerned with evidence of character in the above type of case. The following is only concerned with cases where evidence of character is offered to be used circumstantially; cases where the trier is asked to infer that an individual acted on the occasion under review in accordance with their character as shown by evidence of their reputation or of specific actions performed on other occasions.

The law regards character evidence as relevant to whether a person acted in a certain way on the occasion under review. The law has traditionally decided that there is such a thing as a personality trait or character and that there is a rational and legitimate connection between evidence of a person's character and the proposition that he acted on a particular occasion in conformity with the same, not as determinative of the issue but as having a legitimate influence on reason.[19] Many would disagree with the law's basic assumptions in this area. For them, behaviour on a particular occasion is largely shaped not by the person's antecedents but by the specifics, by the context, of the occasion.[20] Much of what follows then, in discussing the law of evidence as to character, may, in fact, be contrary to the laws of nature but is in accord with the current law.

The common law of evidence concedes the relevance of character and spends its time dealing with when and how the same may be evidenced. Evidence of a person's character is regarded as circumstantial evidence leading legitimately to the conclusion that he or she behaved that way on the occasion being investigated. The following proceeds on the basis that the common law assumptions are justified and that concerns as to their validity should only affect the weight to be attributed to character evidence. Regarding character evidence as relevant does not, of course, guarantee receivability. As with all evidence, the probative worth of character evidence in any particular case may be outweighed by competing considerations such as time, confusion and prejudice and thus character evidence may be excluded, not as irrelevant, but for other reasons.

It is important to remind oneself that character evidence is simply a particular form of circumstantial evidence. Evidence of how a person acted on another occasion is evidence of a circumstance from which we ask the trier of fact to infer that the person acted in a similar fashion on the occasion being litigated. If the evidence is that the person always, invariably, acted in a certain way, the circumstantial evidence is very probative and deserves to be received. We label this as evidence of habit but see it for what it is -a piece of circumstantial evidence, more specific than evidence of the person's general character but differing only in degree and not in kind. If the circumstantial evidence indicates invariable habit the evidence is very powerful. If the evidence is that the person normally acted in that way the circumstantial evidence is less powerful. If the evidence is that he acted in that way occasionally, the court may have concerns that the time necessary to hear the evidence may not be justified given the low probative value. If the evidence is of the person's general character or personality trait, the court recognizes that, even though the person's character or trait has relevance, the probative value may be outweighed by competing considerations and should be excluded. The court recognizes that even so-called "good people" sometimes do bad things and "bad people" do good things. Plumbing the depths of their character may not be worth the time and trouble. Determining

---

19 *R. v. Clarke* (1998), 18 C.R. (5th) 219 (Ont. C.A.).
20 See, *e.g.*, Mendez, "California's New Law on Character Evidence" (1984) 31 U.C.L.A. Rev. 1003.

receivability is thus seen to be a matter for the trial judge's discretion where she weighs probative value against the dangers of consumption of time, confusion of the issues and prejudice to the proper outcome of the trial.

Generally speaking, the character of the plaintiff or defendant in a civil case is not receivable for the purpose of proving that the litigant acted in conformity therewith on the occasion under review.[21] Evidence of character presents special problems in criminal cases when we ask the trier to infer that the accused or the alleged victim in a criminal case acted in conformity with that character.

(a) Evidence of the Accused's Character and Similar Facts

An accused can lead evidence of his good character for the purpose of persuading the trier of fact that he acted in conformity with that character on the occasion under review. Since such evidence is regarded as relevant, and there are no canons of exclusion, the evidence is receivable.[22] If, however, the accused leads evidence of good character, the prosecution is entitled to lead evidence to rebut the same to ensure that the trier of fact is not misled.[23]

There is, however, a canon of exclusion which states that the prosecution may not lead evidence of the accused's bad character for the purpose of persuading the trier that he acted in conformity with that character and that he did the deed alleged. The evidence is regarded as relevant but inadmissible because of the competing consideration of prejudice.[24] Prejudice in this context does not mean that the evidence might increase the chances of conviction but rather that the evidence might be improperly used by the trier of fact. It is one thing for evidence to operate unfortunately for an accused but it is quite another matter for the evidence to operate unfairly. It is the possibility of unfairness that is the concern. The trier who learns of the accused's previous misconduct may view the accused as a bad man, one who deserves punishment regardless of his guilt of the instant offence and may be less critical of the evidence presently marshalled against him concerning the particular incident now complained of.

A chain of reasoning through the accused's disposition to the event is often tenuous in its nature as people can change and dispositions can vary. The canon of exclusion erected by the law of evidence for character evidence

---

21 See *Attorney General v. Radloff* (1854), 156 E.R. 366 (Exch.), at 371. But see "Similar Fact Evidence in Civil Cases" infra.

22 See *R. v. Tarrant* (1981), 63 C.C.C. (2d) 385 (Ont. C.A.), at 388.

23 See, *e.g.*, s. 666 of the *Criminal Code*, R.S.C. 1985, c. C-46. And see generally *R. v. McNamara (No. 1)* (1981), 56 C.C.C. (2d) 193 at 352 (Ont. C.A.).

24 See *R. v. Rowton* (1865), 10 Cox C.C. 25 (Eng. C.C.R.), 38 and *Attorney General v. Hitchcock* (1847), 1 Exch. 91 (Eng. Exch.).

excludes material then which is tenuous in its nature. Such evidence has little probative worth and, when viewed against the possibility of prejudice, deserves exclusion. If, however, the character evidence is not tenuous in its nature, if the accused's conduct is very similar to the incident under review, if it has sufficient relevance, or if it has genuine probative worth when taken together with the other evidence, it may not then be outweighed by considerations of prejudice, and the reason for the canon of exclusion disappears. The first principle of rational fact-finding, that all relevant evidence should be received, then controls and the similar fact evidence should be received. It was out of considerations of fairness, to avoid prejudice, to ensure that the accused is tried for having done a particular bad thing and not for being a bad person, that the law decided to exclude character evidence when tendered by the prosecution.

Rules of admissibility exclude relevant information and therefore require good reason for their operation. Having identified the reason for the canon of exclusion of evidence of bad character tendered by the prosecution, it is only common sense that when the reason for the rule doesn't exist the court should not apply it. If the chance of the evidence having a prejudicial effect is minimal, and the probative value is powerful, the evidence should be received. If the trial judge decides that the evidence won't be used for an improper purpose, that the jury won't just conclude that the accused is a bad man, but rather will use the evidence rationally to decide that he is *the* man alleged, the trial judge will decide the evidence should be received.

The jurisprudence surrounding similar fact evidence has for some years been quite confusing. Very recently however our highest court has brought considerable clarity to the issue.[25] The Supreme Court has decided, consistent with the above text, that similar facts are admissible provided that the probative value outweighs the possibility of prejudice. The Court recognized that a trier might reason through the accused's demonstrated propensity or disposition provided the same is not general but specific.[26]

Before allegedly similar facts can be considered as evidence in the case there must be seen to be a connection between the previous acts and the accused. If the previous acts cannot be tied to the accused they have no relevance at all. Canadian courts have recognized this fact but have yet to clearly articulate an appropriate test. Should the prosecution have to establish beyond a reasonable doubt that the accused committed the earlier acts? On a balance of probabilities? To whose satisfaction? The judge as a preliminary condition of admissibility? The jury, who decides everything at

---

25 See *R. v. Handy* (2002), 1 C.R. (6th) 203 (S.C.C.)

26 See also Delisle, *Batte: Similar Fact Evidence Is a Matter of Propensity*, (2000) 34 C.R. (5th) 240.

the end of the case?[27] The jurisprudence to date has paid little attention to this preliminary condition of admissibility. We can say, at least, that the trial judge must decide that there is some evidence capable of supporting a finding that the accused was implicated in the other activities before the judge proceeds to the next step of determining relevance and probative value versus prejudice.[28]

The test for the reception or rejection of similar fact evidence in a criminal case is simple to articulate if we keep basic principles in mind. The trier who learns of the accused's previous misconduct may view the accused as a bad person and may be less critical of the evidence presently marshalled against him concerning the particular incident now complained of. The law recognizes that reasoning through character can be dangerous as people can change and their dispositions can vary. The law then erects a canon of exclusion for character evidence which has little probative worth, when viewed against the possibility of prejudice. If, however, the character evidence has genuine probative worth and is not outweighed by considerations of prejudice, the reason for the canon of exclusion disappears and the similar fact evidence should be received. The test for reception or rejection is simple to articulate if we keep these basic principles in mind. In terms of its underlying principles, the application of the rule requires only that we measure probative worth against the possibility of prejudice. It is true that given our present jurisprudence a certain formula of words is necessary to pass appellate review but the test is, in actual fact, easy to spell out. Make no mistake. While the test is simple to articulate, the balancing of these competing considerations is one of the most difficult tasks facing a trial judge today.

(b) Manner of Proving Character of the Accused

Until the late nineteenth century, the normal technique of informing the trier of the accused's character, when evidence of character had been ruled admissible, was by the opinions of those who knew him, bolstered at times by their reports of his reputation. That practice was then reversed in the latter part of the nineteenth century and henceforth character witnesses were to testify solely to the person's reputation in the community for the character

---

27 See generally D.M. Tanovich, "Probative Value and the Issue of Proof in Similar Fact Evidence Cases" (1994), 23 C.R. (4th) 157. See *R. v. Ross* (1996), [1996] O.J. No. 1360, 1996 CarswellOnt 1424 (Gen. Div.), *per* Salhany J., announcing a requirement that the judge must "ensure that the allegations clearly establish that a criminal offence has been committed by the accused against that proposed witness."

28 *Sweitzer v. R.* (1982), 68 C.C.C. (2d) 193 (S.C.C.); and *R. v. Millar* (1989), 49 C.C.C. (3d) 193 (Ont. C.A.).

trait under review.[29] That community need not be the person's residential community; it may be the person's reputation among a circle of persons who are familiar with her, perhaps at her workplace.[30]

Relatively recently, the law has fashioned an exception to the general rule, limiting character to reputation, to accommodate psychiatric opinion evidence. Psychiatric opinion evidence is admissible in a criminal case where it would appear that the perpetrator of the crime alleged is a person with an abnormal or unusual propensity or disposition which stamps him as being a member of a special and extraordinary class. In that event, psychiatric evidence may be led by the accused to show that he does not fit within that class or that another person who could have been the perpetrator does fit.[31] The prosecution's ability to lead such evidence — that the accused does fit within the class of people who would commit such a crime — is limited in exactly the same way as the prosecution is limited with respect to the introduction of similar fact evidence.[32]

(c) Character of the Victim

Previous actions of a victim, if known to an accused, may have relevance to the actions of the accused, as knowledge of the same may have caused the accused to act in the way that he did. For example, on a charge of assault, where the defence is self-defence, if the accused had heard that the alleged victim had bashed others on other occasions, that knowledge may be seen by the trier as supporting the reasonableness of the accused's actions. Previous acts of the victim, even though unknown to the accused at the time of the incident, may also have relevance as supporting an inference that the deceased had a propensity to act in that way which made it likely that it resulted in certain conduct on the occasion under review. For example, previous acts of violence by the victim are receivable to show a disposition for violence in the victim and the jury may be invited to infer that the victim acted in conformity with that disposition on the occasion under review. That evidence could then support an accused's evidence that the victim acted on that particular occasion in a life-threatening manner.[33]

Receiving evidence of the victim's previous actions could prejudice the proper outcome of the trial. The trier might conclude, as the result of such evidence, that the complainant's worth as a person is suspect and, accordingly, they might not take their task of carefully analyzing the evidence as

---

29   *R. v. Rowton* (1865), 10 Cox C.C. 25.

30   *R. v. Levasseur* (1987), 56 C.R. (3d) 335 (Alta. C.A.).

31   *R. v. Lupien*, [1970] S.C.R. 263; *R. v. McMillan* (1975), 7 O.R. (2d) 360 (C.A.); and *R. v. Mohan* (1994), 29 C.R. (4th) 243 (S.C.C.).

32   *R. v. Morin*, [1988] 2 S.C.R. 345; and *R. v. Mohan, ibid.*

33   *R. v. Scopelliti, supra*, note 12; and *R. v. Yaeck* (1991), 10 C.R. (4th) 1 (Ont. C.A.).

seriously as they should. The trial judge must carefully assess the probative value of the evidence of the victim's character and ensure that it outweighs the possibility of prejudice to the proper outcome of the trial.[34]

The character evidence of the victim may be in the form of reputation, in the form of evidence of specific instances of previous conduct or by evidence of psychiatric opinion.

(d) Character of the Victim in Sexual Assault Cases

The position at common law was that evidence could be led: (1) of the alleged victim's general reputation and moral character, and (2) concerning sexual intercourse between herself and the accused on other occasions. No evidence could be called by the accused concerning sexual intercourse between the complainant and other men. The law regarded evidence of (1) and (2) as relevant to the material issue of consent but evidence of sexual intercourse between the complainant and other men as irrelevant to the issue of consent. The alleged victim, however, could be asked about instances of sexual intercourse with persons other than the accused as the same was seen as relevant to credibility. If the alleged victim denied such activity she could not be contradicted because such contradictory evidence would be in violation of a rule of evidence which forbids the introduction of evidence of collateral facts; evidence which goes solely to credibility. At common law, the victim's reputation for promiscuity was also seen as relevant to her credibility as well as directly relevant to the issue of consent.[35]

In 1992, the *Criminal Code* was amended:

276. (1) In proceedings in respect of [sexual offences], evidence that the complainant has engaged in sexual activity, whether with the accused or with any other person, is not admissible to support an inference that, by reason of the sexual nature of that activity, the complainant

(a) is more likely to have consented to the sexual activity that forms the subject-matter of the charge; or
(b) is less worthy of belief.

(2) In proceedings in respect of an offence referred to in subsection (1), no evidence shall be adduced by or on behalf of the accused that the complainant has engaged in sexual activity other than the sexual activity that forms the subject-matter of the charge, whether with the accused or with any other person, unless the judge, provincial court judge or justice determines, . . . that the evidence

---

34 See *R. v. Scopelliti, ibid.*
35 See *R. v. Krausz* (1973), 57 Cr. App. R. 466 (C.C.A.); and *R. v. Basken* (1974), 21 C.C.C. (2d) 321 (Sask. C.A.).

(a) is of specific instances of sexual activity;

(b) is relevant to an issue at trial; and

(c) has significant probative value that is not substantially outweighed by the danger of prejudice to the proper administration of justice.

277. In proceedings in respect of [sexual offences], evidence of sexual reputation, whether general or specific, is not admissible for the purpose of challenging or supporting the credibility of the complainant.

The legislation also provided a detailed procedure for determining whether the evidence could be received under subsection (2).

On a trial of sexual assault, receiving evidence of the complainant's previous sexual history has the potential to prejudice the proper outcome of the trial. The trier may give the evidence an exaggerated probative value on the issue of consent. Alternatively, the trier might conclude, as the result of such evidence, that the complainant's worth as a person is suspect, and accordingly they might not take their task of carefully analyzing the evidence as seriously as they should; they might not see a conviction as important as it might be seen with respect to another victim. On the other hand, a blanket exclusion of such evidence could do an injustice as it could interfere with an accused's right to make full answer and defence; the accused's rights in this regard are guaranteed by the common law, and in Canada by the *Criminal Code*[36] and section 7 of the *Canadian Charter of Rights and Freedoms.*[37]

To draw the appropriate line which will ensure a fair trial and at the same time protect the legitimate interests of both the complainant and the accused, the evidentiary provisions enacted by the Canadian Parliament have been read subject to an overriding discretion in the trial judge to receive evidence of the complainant's previous sexual history when the trial judge determines that the probative value of the same outweighs the possibility of prejudice to the proper outcome of the trial. So long as the inference from past to present behaviour does not rest on highly dubious beliefs about "women who do" and "women who don't", evidence of the complainant's previous sexual activity, with the accused or with another, will probably not be foreclosed by s. 276.[38] If the relevance is regarded as rational and strong, the court will probably receive.

There is, of course, a fundamental and unavoidable problem resident in the determination of relevance as required by the legislation. As we've

---

36 Sections 276(3)(a), 650(3) and 802(1).

37 *Constitution Act, 1982*, R.S.C. 1985, App. II, No. 44.

38 See *R. v. Osolin* (1993), 26 C.R. (4th) 1 (S.C.C.); and *R. v. Ecker* (1995), 37 C.R. (4th) 1 (Sask. C.A.) and *R. v. Darrach* (2000), 36 C.R. (5th) 223 (S.C.C.). See also, Delisle, *Adoption Sub-silentio, of the Paciocco Solution to Rape Shield Laws*, (2001) 36 C.R. (5th) 254.

seen, it is the trial judge who needs to answer the question of whether the evidence of previous sexual history makes the proposition for which it is tendered any more likely than would be the case if the evidence was not introduced. It is for the trial judge, if he determines the evidence to be relevant, to determine how probative the evidence is in comparison to competing considerations. The law of evidence does not furnish an answer. Relevance is not dictated by the law but by common sense and experience. The judge decides, based on his or her common sense and experience. The pre-eminent question is whether the judge's common sense and experience in this area mirrors that of the community. While this problem is present in all determinations of relevance, the problem is seen to be particularly acute in sexual assault cases. This is because, historically, the law has accepted as relevant evidence in sexual assault cases material which is now seen to be clearly irrelevant. This area of the law has been particularly susceptible to the utilization of stereotype in determinations of relevance.[39]

(e) Similar Fact Evidence in Civil Cases

There are far fewer reported civil cases involving the problem of similar facts than criminal cases. In those reported, the approach is usually the same. The same underlying concerns are expressed. The defendant came to deal with one allegation of misconduct and it is not fair to call on him to defend all past allegations. He might be taken by surprise and he might be unfairly prejudiced in the eyes of the jury by evidence of his previous conduct. Again, a suitable answer lies in the discretion of the trial judge to weigh these competing considerations against probative value.[40]

The plaintiff sues for damages for injuries sustained from a fall on the defendant's premises. The plaintiff maintains that the fall was caused by the overly slick tile floor in the defendant's foyer. The defendant denies negligence on his part and maintains that the fall was caused by the plaintiff's own awkwardness. The defendant avers that he was unaware that the floor was slick. The plaintiff offers evidence that one, two, three or four others have fallen in the defendant's foyer. The number and the similarity of circumstances will affect probative value. The previous happenings could be relevant to whether the fall was caused by the slippery floor and could also be relevant to the issue of whether the defendant had notice of a dangerous condition on his property. The judge worries that if the jury hears of others being hurt on the defendant's premises they might be moved to

---

39 See Justice L'Heureux-Dubé in *R. v. Seaboyer*, [1991] 2 S.C.R. 577.
40 See *McWilliams v. Arrol*, [1962] 1 All E.R. 623 (H.L.); *Mood Music v. DeWolfe*, [1976] 2 W.L.R. 452 (C.A.); and *MacDonald v. Canada Kelp Co.* (1973), 39 D.L.R. (3d) 617 (B.C. C.A.).

award damages whether or not the jury was persuaded that there actually was negligence in the case being reviewed. The judge must exercise a discretion in determining whether to admit the evidence. Probative value versus prejudice and time, akin to the criminal law process. The judge might decide to admit as relevant notice to the defendant but not on the issue of whether the injury was actually caused by a dangerous condition. Or he might decide to exclude altogether.

In *Teskey,*[41] a weekly newspaper published an advertisement placed by O. that contained an attack on the plaintiffs. O. had previously made similar attacks. The plaintiffs sued for libel. The trial judge told the jury that the defence of fair comment would be excluded by malice, which he defined as ill-will, spite or indirect motive. The jury awarded substantial damages to the plaintiffs. The defendant appealed. At the outset of the trial, a motion had been made by counsel for the plaintiffs for the admission of approximately 160 pages of clippings from the newspaper from 1975 to 1983 consisting of editorials and reports of statements made by or about O. and the controversies they had generated. The learned trial judge ruled that this material was admissible. On appeal, the defendant argued that while she had no objection to the admission of any clippings dealing with the plaintiffs, she did object to the admission of what she called similar fact evidence in the material relating to allegations of misconduct by O. against other individuals. The Court analyzed the evidence in accordance with doctrine taken from criminal cases. The Court noted that such evidence was not admissible to show, from past conduct, a person's disposition to commit certain types of acts. But, again looking to the pigeonhole list often quoted in criminal cases, the Court noted that such evidence was admissible if it was relevant, *inter alia*, to show malice. If the evidence was relevant to malice, the evidence was only admissible if its probative value was not outweighed by the prejudice caused by its admission. The Court of Appeal concluded that the trial judge had properly applied the principles in admitting the evidence. There was evidence to support a finding of malice against O. and that defeated the defence of fair comment. The reader might be moved to ask how this evidence went to prove malice save and except by illustrating O.'s disposition.

6. The Relevance Rules

Certain factual situations so regularly occur that the law of evidence, applying the above general principles, has created what might be referred

---

41   *Teskey v. Canadian Newspapers Co.* (1989), 68 O.R. (2d) 737 (C.A.), leave to appeal to
      S.C.C. refused (1990), 37 O.A.C. 396 (note) (S.C.C.).

to as relevance rules of thumb because of the consistent treatment in the courts.

(a) Evidence of Flight

In a criminal case, it is commonly understood that an accused's flight from the scene of a crime is evidence that the accused believed he was guilty of the crime. From that inference another inference, that the accused was in fact guilty, naturally flows. An inference of guilt then may be drawn from circumstantial evidence such as flight from the scene of a crime or the fabrication of lies or the destruction of evidence relating to the offence in question. Evidence of flight is therefore commonly admitted as relevant to the material issue. However, in charging a jury, a trial judge must take care to ensure that evidence of flight is not misused. There is always a danger that a jury might leap from such evidence too quickly to a conclusion of guilt if not properly instructed. The probative worth of an inference of consciousness of guilt of the particular crime being investigated may be tenuous in comparison to the possibility of prejudice resident in the jury giving the evidence more weight than it deserves. There may be other reasons accounting for the flight.[42]

(b) Subsequent Repairs and Settlement Offers

In a civil suit for damages, alleging negligence in the failure of the accused to maintain his property in a safe condition, it is arguable that any repairs to the property made by the defendant subsequent to the accident are relevant to culpability. As with an accused's flight from the scene of a crime, one can maintain that the fact of the subsequent repairs indicates an awareness, a belief, in the defendant that his premises were unsafe at the time of the accident. From that belief it is rational to infer that in fact the premises were unsafe. Our courts used to exclude this evidence on the basis that receiving the same might discourage property owners from properly maintaining their property. More recently, however, our courts have rejected this as a fallacious argument and have signalled a willingness to receive the same.[43]

If the defendant property owner in the above hypothetical offered to pay damages to the plaintiff to settle the controversy, such an offer might also be seen to be relevant to the issue of negligence. Again, the chain of

---

42 See *R. v. Arcangioli*, [1994] 1 S.C.R. 129. Compare *R. v. Thurston* (2001), 43 C.R. (5th) 153 (Ont. C.A.).

43 See *Algoma Central Railway v. Herb Fraser & Associates Ltd.* (1988), 66 O.R. (2d) 330 (Div. Ct.); and *Canadian Pacific Railway v. Calgary (City)* (1966), 59 D.L.R. (2d) 642 (Alta. C.A.).

reasoning is that such an offer indicated a belief in the defendant that he was negligent and from such a belief we could properly infer that he was in fact negligent. But, again, much would depend on the circumstances. Another explanation might be forthcoming: the defendant, a lifelong friend of his neighbour plaintiff, without any real belief in his own negligence, might have made the gesture out of feelings of friendship.[44] In such a case, the evidence would be lacking in relevance. In any event, the courts might exclude such evidence, even if they concluded that there was relevance, on the basis that they want to encourage settlements to avoid congestion in the courts; if such offers were routinely received in evidence they might not be as forthcoming.[45]

(c) Liability Insurance

Is there relevance in a civil suit for negligence that the defendant was insured against liability? One could argue that if a person took out insurance against any liability flowing from his activities, such person might be less careful in carrying out those activities, as he is fully protected from loss, and from there infer that on the particular occasion under review he was negligent. One could argue that the probative worth of such evidence is tenuous and that being insured actually marks the person as one of those cautious and careful individuals who take all appropriate precautions against risk. In any event, our courts have decided that should any evidence be led from which a jury might reasonably conclude that the defendant is insured the jury should be dispensed with and the trial continued without a jury. The reason is obvious. The concern is that a jury will be more likely to return a verdict that the defendant was negligent when they learn that the defendant will not personally have to pay any award and that damages will be payable by a large faceless corporation.[46]

(d) Judicial Findings

Suppose a motor vehicle accident occurs. Such an accident produces criminal and civil consequences. Suppose the driver of one of the vehicles is later convicted of criminal negligence in the operation of a motor vehicle following a plea of not guilty. Suppose the other driver now sues. Is the plaintiff entitled to prove the earlier conviction for the purpose of establishing the facts on which the conviction was based? Is it relevant? Suppose an accused is convicted of murdering his wife. The accused later sues to recover

---

44 *Walmsley v. Humenick*, [1954] 2 D.L.R. 232 (B.C. S.C.).
45 See Privilege for Without Prejudice Negotiations, *infra*, Chapter 6.
46 See, *e.g.*, *Theakston v. Bowhey*, [1951] S.C.R. 679.

the proceeds of his deceased wife's estate. Can the estate resist his claims and prove the previous conviction as evidence that he was the author of the death and therefore cannot recover? Is it relevant?

Our courts have now decided that previous convictions of a criminal offence are relevant and therefore receivable in a subsequent civil suit for the purpose of establishing the facts on which the conviction was based.[47] It is to be noted that the previous judicial finding is not conclusive on the point; it is simply seen to be relevant.[48]

Suppose in each of the above scenarios the accused had earlier pleaded guilty. Our courts have decided that a plea of guilty amounts to an admission and therefore evidences a belief in that person that he was guilty as charged; from that belief it is seen to be fair to infer that the person did do the things alleged.[49] Again, the plea is regarded as relevant and therefore receivable as evidence but it is not conclusive as to the matter. Our courts recognize that there can be reasons for a plea other than a belief in guilt.

---

47 *Demeter v. British Pacific Life Insurance Co.* (1985), 48 O.R. (2d) 266 (C.A.).
48 For statutory provisions authorizing the receipt of previous convictions in subsequent civil suits, see R.S.A. 2000, c. A-18, s. 26; R.S.B.C. 1996, c. 124, s. 71.
49 *English v. Richmond,* [1956] S.C.R. 383.

2

Manner of Proof

1. Introduction

It is rare that we can be certain regarding the existence of any past historical fact. In the courtroom we are in the hands of witnesses who seek to describe, often at a much later time, their earlier interpretation of the material events. If we required certainty in our judicial decision-making, decisions would be few and far between. Our procedural law, our law of evidence, accommodates this fact by providing the device of burdens of proof. A trier of fact is entitled to find for a party, though not certain that the facts occurred as alleged, if the trier is persuaded to a belief that the party's version is probably true, in civil cases, or is persuaded beyond a reasonable doubt, in criminal cases.

2. The Persuasive and the Evidential Burden of Proof

There are two legal burdens which need to be distinguished: the persuasive burden and the evidential burden. The former has to do with persuading the trier and the latter has to do with leading evidence concerning the matter. The law of evidence has nothing to do with the allocation of these burdens. The law of evidence does not determine responsibility regarding either the leading of evidence or regarding who should persuade whom. Rather, the law of pleadings and substantive law dictate the same. The law of evidence supplies the tools for the task but the policy decision of who will bear what burden is left to other disciplines. The following discusses the substance of the tools provided.

When a party has the persuasive burden with respect to a proposition concerning which the parties are at odds, we say that that party will lose the case if, at the end of the day, he hasn't persuaded the trier of fact to his point of view. For example, if the plaintiff in a civil suit satisfies the jury that his view of the proposition is correct, he wins. If, on the other hand, the jury concludes that the question ought to be clearly answered in favour of the defendant, then the plaintiff loses. But, if the jury in a civil case is in a real state of doubt at the end of the case the plaintiff has failed to satisfy his burden of proof and he loses.[1] The law demands that the plaintiff (or the prosecutor in a criminal case) persuade the trier to a real belief in his proposition. The persuasive burden is sometimes referred to as the legal, ultimate, major or primary burden.

The persuasive burden never shifts. The plaintiff or the prosecutor is saddled with this burden at the outset of the case and it never leaves his or her shoulders. It is only discharged when the jury comes back in and says "We find for the plaintiff" or "Guilty, your honour." The persuasive burden is to be distinguished from the non-legal, tactical burden. A newcomer to the case asks a spectator how the case is going. The spectator says it's going pretty well for the plaintiff, or for the defendant, and that if the other side doesn't do something it will probably lose. The other side has the tactical burden. There is no legal consequence that flows from failure to discharge the tactical burden; it is simply that as a matter of tactics it would be wise to lead some evidence or risk failure.[2]

The evidential burden, a lesser burden than the persuasive, rests on any party who wants a certain proposition to be considered by the trier of fact. The proposition which the party sees as important will not be open for consideration by the trier of fact unless the trial judge determines there is some evidence in the case to make it a real issue. The party is not entitled to make submissions to the jury unless there is, in the evidence, a basis for the same. Otherwise the decision would be speculative and not rational. The evidential burden is sometimes referred to as the minor or secondary burden.

The evidential burden, when resting on the shoulders of the plaintiff or prosecutor, is sometimes referred to as the duty of going forward or the duty of passing the judge. There is a legal effect if the plaintiff or prosecutor fails to discharge this burden. If the trial judge determines that there is insufficient evidence on which a properly instructed jury could reasonably conclude in favour of the plaintiff or prosecutor, the trial judge will not permit the trier to consider the case. Using the current jargon, the plaintiff in a civil case will be non-suited; in a criminal case, the trial judge will direct a verdict of acquittal for the accused.

The evidential burden resting on the shoulders of the defendant in a civil case or on the accused in a criminal case operates to foreclose consideration of a defence unless there is evidence in the case which gives the defence an air of reality. Suppose a criminal case. The prosecution and the defence have signalled to the trial judge that all the evidence they choose to lead in the case has been led. The trial judge asks the accused for assistance as to how he should charge the jury. It would be unthinkable for the accused

---

1 See generally *Abrath v. North Eastern Railway* (1883), 11 Q.B. 79 (C.A.), *per* Brett M.R.
2 See, *e.g.*, *Snell v. Farrell*, [1990] 2 S.C.R. 311 at 329.

to ask the judge to tell the jury that they might acquit if they found that the accused was drunk at the time of the incident and therefore incapable of forming the necessary intent; that he is entitled to be acquitted if they find he was acting in self-defence; or that they might acquit if they find that there were grounds of duress excusing his actions, if there had been no evidence led in the case as to intoxication, self-defence or duress. A defence should not be put to the jury if a reasonable jury properly instructed would have been unable to acquit on the basis of the evidence tendered in support of that defence. On the other hand, if a reasonable jury properly instructed could acquit on the basis of the evidence tendered with regard to that defence, then it must be put to the jury. It is for the trial judge to decide whether the evidence is sufficient to warrant putting a defence to a jury as this is a question of law alone. The trial judge needs to determine if there is an air of reality to the suggested defence. There is thus a two-step procedure which must be followed. First, the trial judge must review all the evidence and decide if it is sufficient to warrant putting the defence to the jury. Second, if the evidence meets that threshold, the trial judge must put the defence to the jury, which in turn will weigh it and decide whether it raises a reasonable doubt. The evidence need not come from sources other than the accused but there must be something in the evidence, from the accused's testimony or elsewhere, that is capable of supporting the accused's or defendant's position.[3] If there is no such evidence in support, it would be irrational for the trier to consider the defence. A verdict not based on the evidence would be perverse.

The case of *Woolmington* provides us with a good vehicle for seeing the distinction between the two burdens.[4] Reginald Woolmington was convicted of murdering his bride. Reggie testified. The shooting was admitted but Reginald said it was an accident. The trial judge told the jury that, once the killing was proved, a persuasive burden fell on the shoulders of the accused and the accused had to prove that the killing was an accident. The accused had to satisfy the trier, had to persuade the trier, that his proposition of accidental death was the true version of what happened that day. The House of Lords said no. The Lords said that the prosecution had to prove both the killing and the requisite mental state of malice. The prosecution had to prove all of the material ingredients of the offence. Once the Crown had proved the killing there was evidence on which the jury might find guilt but they were not required to do so. There was no burden on the accused to prove his innocence, to prove the absence of a material ingredient. The accused was entitled to be acquitted at the end of the day if the trier of fact

---

3   *R. v. Osolin* (1993), 26 C.R. (4th) 1 (S.C.C.); and *R. v. Park* (1995), 39 C.R. (4th) 287 (S.C.C.).
4   *Woolmington v. D.P.P.*, [1935] A.C. 462 (H.L.).

had a reasonable doubt concerning the existence of any material ingredient. His testimony concerning accident satisfied his evidential burden and, if the jury had a reasonable doubt as to whether the killing had been by accident, Woolmington deserved to be acquitted.

It is important to recognize that the imposition of the evidential burden regarding accident in *Woolmington* does not mean that the accused must himself testify, nor indeed call any evidence. It is enough for the accused to point out that there is evidence in the prosecution's case which will support the doubt. For example, there may have been a statement made to the police during the course of the investigation which was partly inculpatory and partly exculpatory: "I did it, but I was drunk." That statement when introduced by the Crown becomes evidence in the case and the defence might point to it and ask the judge to charge the jury to consider the possibility that the accused did not have the capacity to form the requisite intent.[5]

3. Facts Peculiarly Within the Knowledge of the Accused

We have said that the law of evidence does not allocate burdens of proof but that the same is done by the substantive law and the law of pleadings. There is, however, a "doctrine" which has crept into the law and, if its boundaries are not kept, the doctrine can be exceedingly dangerous.

In an old English case, the accused was charged with having game in his possession.[6] The statute provided a number of exceptions and qualifications and the accused argued that before a conviction could be had the prosecution had to negative each. The Court decided that this would place an intolerable burden on the prosecution and, because the matter was a fact peculiarly within the knowledge of the accused, it lay with him to establish. In later cases, where the statute provided that it was an offence to do something without a licence, the courts decided that since the possession of a licence was a fact peculiarly within the knowledge of the accused it was for him to establish.[7] All of this seems relatively sound. If a defendant in Ontario today is prosecuted for fishing without a licence, and there are thousands of licence-issuing authorities within the province, it seems sensible that the accused prove his licence as it might be well nigh impossible for the prosecution to negative and it's quite a simple task for the accused. Even here, however, placing an evidential burden rather than a persuasive

---

5 See *R. v. Latour*, [1951] S.C.R. 19 at 23.
6 *R. v. Turner* (1816), 105 E. R. 1026.
7 See, *e.g.*, *John v. Humphreys*, [1955] 1 All E.R. 793.

would be sufficient, although with licences it comes to pretty much the same thing.

But, if we don't restrict the application of the principle it could relieve the prosecution of its normal burden of proof and make a mockery of the presumption of innocence.[8] There are reported cases which, invoking this doctrine, placed the persuasive burden on the accused: on a charge of careless driving, to prove that he was not driving carelessly[9] since whether he was or not was a matter peculiarly within his knowledge; on a charge under the *Criminal Code* of dangerous driving, to prove that he was not driving dangerously;[10] and on a charge of breaching occupational safety legislation to prove that the person who did the prohibited thing was not subject to the authority of the accused.[11] If this doctrine is not narrowly confined the presumption of innocence could be seriously impaired. In a murder prosecution, where a killing by the accused was established, there would be a burden on the accused of establishing that he did not intend to cause death, as nothing could be more peculiarly within the knowledge of the accused than whether or not he meant to cause death. The doctrine must be kept within the bounds of its origins.

4. The Measure of the Burden of Persuasion

There is said to be a marked distinction between the degree of satisfaction that is necessary in order for the trier of fact to be persuaded in a civil case and that which is necessary in a criminal case. Traditionally we say that in a civil case the trier needs only to be persuaded on a balance of probabilities, by a preponderance of the evidence,[12] whereas in a criminal case the trier must be persuaded beyond a reasonable doubt.[13] It is understandable if one should ask whether that is really true. One might logically conclude that a trier is satisfied or not, has a belief in the proponent's position or does not. And the trier's necessary degree of satisfaction to achieve that belief rests not on the characterization of the issue as civil or criminal but rather on the trier's awareness of the consequences that will flow from his decision. How much rides on the decision? Nevertheless, the formula of words, balance of probabilities or preponderance of the evidence in a civil case and beyond a reasonable doubt continues in force. Our courts say that these standards do not vary. In applying these standards, however, the courts

8   *R. v. Billet* (1952), 105 C.C.C. 169 (B.C. S.C.).

9   *R. v. McIver,* [1965] 2 O.R. 475 (C.A.).

10 *R. v. Peda* (1968), [1969] 1 O.R. 90 (C.A.).

11 *R. v. Strand Electric Ltd.,* [1969] 1 O.R. 190 (C.A.).

12 *Smith v. Smith,* [1952] 2 S.C.R. 312.

13 *Woolmington v. D.P.P., supra,* note 4.

recognize that a trier will scrutinize the evidence with greater care if there are serious allegations[14] and that there may be variations in the amount of evidence required to satisfy either standard.[15] The reader is excused if he or she sees this as a semantic quibble.

It is wrong, reversible error, if the trial judge tells the jury that proof beyond a reasonable doubt are ordinary everyday words. The Supreme Court recently summarized what should be said and what should not be said about reasonable doubt:

It should be explained that:

the standard of proof beyond a reasonable doubt is inextricably intertwined with that principle fundamental to all criminal trials, the presumption of innocence;

the burden of proof rests on the prosecution throughout the trial and never shifts to the accused;

a reasonable doubt is not a doubt based upon sympathy or prejudice; rather, it is based upon reason and common sense;

it is logically connected to the evidence or absence of evidence;

it does not involve proof to an absolute certainty; it is not proof beyond any doubt nor is it an imaginary or frivolous doubt; and

more is required than proof that the accused is probably guilty, a jury which concludes only that the accused is probably guilty must acquit

On the other hand, certain references to the required standard of proof should be avoided.

For example:

describing the term "reasonable doubt" as an ordinary expression which has no special meaning in the criminal law context;

inviting jurors to apply to the task before them the same standard of proof that they apply to important, or even the most important, decisions in their own lives;

equating proof 'beyond a reasonable doubt', 'to proof', '.to a moral certainty',;

qualifying the word ".doubt" with adjectives other than "reasonable", such as 'serious", substantial" or "haunting", which may mislead the jury; and

instructing jurors that they may convict if they are ' .sure' , that the accused is guilty, before providing them with a proper definition as to the meaning of the words "beyond a reasonable doubt".

---

14 *Continental Insurance Co. v. Dalton Cartage Ltd.*, [1982] 1 S.C.R. 164 at 170.

15 *R. v. R. (R.L.)* (1988), 65 C.R. (3d) 235 (Ont. C.A.).

A charge which is consistent with the principles set out in these reasons will suffice regardless of the particular words used by the trial judge.[16]

In determining guilt in a criminal case, in determining whether the trier is satisfied beyond a reasonable doubt, it is wrong, reversible error for the judge to tell the trier to choose between competing versions.[17] To do so is to weaken the standard. The trier must be advised that if the evidence of the accused is believed he is entitled to an acquittal. If the testimony of the accused is not believed but the trier is left in a state of reasonable doubt by it, the accused is entitled to be acquitted. Even if the trier is not left in a state of doubt by the evidence of the accused, the trier must ask himself whether, on the basis of the evidence which he does accept, he is convinced beyond a reasonable doubt of the accused's guilt.[18]

The requisite standard of proof is applicable at the end of the case and is to be applied only in answer to the question of whether on all the evidence the trier is satisfied or not. The standard is not to be applied to each piece of evidence that goes to make up the case. While it may appear sensible that a trier needs to be satisfied as to the existence of each piece of evidence to the same standard as is applicable to the case as a whole, it has been decided that the function of the standard of proof is not the weighing of individual items of evidence but the determination of the ultimate issue.[19]

5. The Rule in *Hodge's Case*

This "rule" came to us in Canada as the result of our reading, or mis-reading, of an old English case.[20] In that case, the Court was dealing with a murder. The evidence against the accused was circumstantial in nature. In charging the jury, the trial judge told them that they could only find guilt if they were satisfied "not only that the circumstances were consistent with his having committed the act, but they must also be satisfied that the facts were such as to be inconsistent with any other rational conclusion than that the prisoner was the guilty person." It now seems clear that this formula of words was not intended to lay down a new rule of law but rather was simply to offer advice to the jury about how they might be satisfied beyond a reasonable doubt in cases where the evidence was circumstantial.[21] Never-

---

16 See *R. v. Lifchus* (1997), amended (1998), 120 C.C.C. (3d) vi (S.C.C.) 9 C.R. (5th) 1 (S.C.C.).

17 See *R. v. Nadeau* (1984), 42 C.R. (3d) 305 (S.C.C.).

18 *R. v. W. (D.)* (1991), 3 C.R. (4th) 302 (S.C.C.); and *R. v. S. (W.D.)* (1994), 34 C.R. (4th) 1 (S.C.C.).

19 See *R. v. Morin*, [1988] 2 S.C.R. 345.

20 *Hodge's Case* (1838), 168 E.R. 1136.

21 *R. v. McGreevy* (1972), [1973] 1 All E.R. 503 at 508-511 (H.L.).

theless, it was viewed by our courts as raising the standard of proof in circumstantial evidence cases to a standard higher than beyond a reasonable doubt and the trial judge was obliged, as a matter of law, in such cases to utter this formula.[22] Thankfully our courts have now recognized the error of their ways and the *Hodge* formula is no longer an inexorable rule of law in Canada.[23] The formula now, not a rule of law, remains a good illustration of how a trier may or may not be satisfied beyond a reasonable doubt in criminal cases based on circumstantial evidence.

6. The Measure of the Evidential Burden

We noted above that the evidential burden resting on a defendant or an accused, necessary to a consideration of their position, was to ensure that there was evidence in the case, led by plaintiff, prosecutor or accused, which gave an air of reality as to its existence. Now we examine the evidential burden entertained by the Crown in a criminal case or by the plaintiff in a civil case.

The evidential burden entertained by the plaintiff or Crown is sometimes referred to as the duty of passing the judge. The plaintiff or Crown must first persuade the judge that his or her case warrants consideration by the jury. It will eventually be for the jury to decide if they are satisfied on a balance of probabilities or satisfied beyond a reasonable doubt, but first the proponent must persuade the judge that there is sufficient evidence, which, if believed, will permit a jury to rationally conclude in favour of the plaintiff or the Crown. The judge is there to confine the jury to act within the parameters of rationality. We don't want to interfere with the jury's ultimate task, but we want to ensure that the opponent is not called on to respond to the case unnecessarily.

The question for the judge is whether there is any evidence upon which a reasonable jury properly instructed *could* return a verdict of guilty. Note the emphasis on the word "could". It will be for the jury to decide if they "would" decide in favour of the plaintiff or the prosecutor. It is for the judge to decide if they rationally *could.* When the trial judge does that assessment, should she incorporate the standard of proof? Should she say then, in a criminal case, "could the jury reasonably be satisfied beyond a reasonable doubt?" It seems logical to incorporate the standard.[24] Otherwise we would

---

22 See, *e.g., R. v. Mitchell* (1964), 46 D.L.R. (2d) 384 deciding the formula was not applicable to proof of mental state because that standard was too high; proof beyond a reasonable doubt would do.

23 *R. v. Cooper* (1977), 74 D.L.R. (3d) 731 at 746 (S.C.C.).

24 For an example of incorporation, see *R. v. Nelles* (1982), 16 C.C.C. (3d) 97 (Ont. Prov. Ct.).

have the anomaly of the trial judge leaving a case to the jury and charging them that they are not to find for the plaintiff or prosecutor unless satisfied to the requisite standard although the trial judge has himself decided that it would be irrational to conclude to the requisite standard. Nevertheless, the bulk of the jurisprudence is to the contrary.[25]

Recent decisions of our highest court have emphasized that when the trial judge makes his determination as to whether a trier of fact could rationally conclude in favour of the proponent of the case he is not to make any assessments as to the credibility of the proponent's witnesses.[26] In *Mezzo*,[27] the accused was charged with rape. The accused did not contest the fact that the victim had been raped. He took issue only with her identification of him as her assailant. At the close of the Crown's case the trial judge, concerned as to the quality of the identification evidence, granted a motion for a directed verdict of acquittal. The Supreme Court held this to be error. According to the Court, the trial judge had disregarded the division of duties between a judge and a jury. It was for the judge to rule on questions of law and for the jury to decide questions of fact. Questions concerning credibility were to be decided by the trier of fact. Perhaps more problematic is our court's assertion that the trial judge is also prohibited from weighing the evidence. In *Monteleone*,[28] the accused was charged with arson. The evidence was entirely circumstantial. The premises were owned by the accused. There was evidence to place him at the scene shortly before the fire started. At the close of the Crown's case, the trial judge acceded to a defence motion for a directed verdict of acquittal. The Supreme Court decided the trial judge had erred and said "it is not open to a judge in a jury trial to consider the weight of the evidence." How a judge is to determine whether a trier could rationally conclude in a proponent's favour without assessing the weight of the case is left unexplained.[29]

The anomaly produced by the early jurisprudence seems now to have been corrected. In a unanimous decision the Court now has said that there is permitted a certain limited weighing function for the trial judge. In *R. v. Arcuri*[30] the Court dealt with the task of a judge on a preliminary inquiry determining whether there was sufficient evidence to commit an accused to

25 See, for example, *R. v. Syms* (1979), 4 C.C.C. (2d) 338 (Ont. C.A.). But compare *R. v. Comba,* [1938] 3 D.L.R. 719 (S.C.C.). But see McLachlin, J. in *R. v. Charemski* (1998), 15 C.R. (5th) 1 (S.C.C.) advocating the inclusion of the standard.

26 *United States v. Sheppard* (1976), 30 C.C.C. (2d) 424 (S.C.C.).

27 *R. v. Mezzo* (1985), 52 C.R. (3d) 113 (S.C.C.).

28 *R. v. Monteleone* (1987), 59 C.R. (3d) 97 (S.C.C.).

29 See D.M. Tanovich, "Monteleone's Legacy: Confusing Sufficient with Weight" (1994), 27 C.R. (4th) 174.

30 (2001), 44 C.R. (5th) 213 (S.C.C.). See Delisle, *Limited Weighing of Circumstantial Evidence,* (2001) 44 C.R. (5th) 227.

stand his trial. That test is recognized to be the same as the test on directed verdict application.[31] The Court noted that if the evidence for the prosecution was direct evidence concerning each and every element of the offence the trial judge's function was very limited since he was not permitted to make any determinations as to credibility. However, if any of the elements of the offence were evidenced by circumstantial evidence there was a role for the trial judge. In that case the judge needs to assess the legitimacy of the inferences necessary to guilt; the judge weighs the evidence in the sense of assessing whether the evidence is reasonably capable of supporting the inferences the prosecution wants the jury to draw.

In a criminal matter, at the close of the prosecution's case, the accused may make an application for a directed verdict of acquittal. The trial judge is obliged to rule on that application when it is made.[32] In a civil case, the defendant at the close of the plaintiff's case may apply for a non-suit. On that application being made the trial judge will ask the defendant whether he intends to call any evidence. If the defendant says no, the trial judge is then assured that all the evidence is in and she will rule on the application. If the defendant says that he intends to lead evidence the trial judge will reserve her decision on the non-suit application until the defendant has led his evidence and will take the defendant's evidence into account when reaching a decision on the non-suit application.[33]

7. Presumptions

To establish a material fact a party may lead circumstantial evidence concerning the same hoping that the trier of fact will infer the material fact. Presumptions in the law of evidence are devices which effect a legal consequence whereby the trier is required to infer a presumed fact when other basic facts are proved if the party against whom the presumption operates fails to do something prescribed by law. It bears emphasis that when a presumption operates a legal result is compelled and not just permitted. It is one thing to say to a trier of fact that it is permissible to infer the material fact from certain circumstantial evidence; it is quite another, distinct thing to say to the trier that he must infer the material fact. Presumptions are statutorily or judicially directed to accommodate some extrinsic policy consideration.

---

31 See e.g. *United States v. Sheppard* supra f.n. 26.
32 *R. v. Angelantoni* (1975), 31 C.R.N.S. 342 at 345 (Ont. C.A.).
33 *Ontario v. O.P.S.E.U.* (1990), 37 O.A.C. 218 (Div. Ct.); and *Bank of Montreal v. Horan* (1986), 54 O.R. (2d) 757 (H.C.).

(a) **False Presumptions**

The term "presumption" is legitimately used only when the matter to be presumed risks the possibility of rebuttal by the adversary doing something in response. A presumption is, by definition, rebuttable. It is not uncommon, however, to see our Legislature refer to "conclusive presumptions". For example "a place that is found to be equipped with a slot machine shall be conclusively presumed to be a common gaming house."[34] In truth this is not a presumptive device; rather it is a statement of substantive law. To minimize confusion stemming from the overuse of the term it would be far better if the Legislature simply provided that "a place that is found to be equipped with a slot machine is a common gaming house." The effect is the same and much more straightforward.

Sometimes, what is simply a permissible inference is labelled a presumption. For example, it is sometimes said that a person is presumed to intend the natural consequences of his acts. This is error. To be consistent with the requirement that the prosecution has the burden of proving its case beyond a reasonable doubt the jury needs to be advised that while they may infer an intention from the doing of an act there is no requirement that they must do so. They may, but there is no must about it.[35] It does not avoid criticism if such a so-called presumption is referred to as a presumption of fact as opposed to a presumption of law, or as a permissive presumption, although our jurisprudence does frequently use this misleading language.[36]

It is sometimes said that a person who is found in possession of goods which were recently stolen, in the absence of an explanation that might reasonably be true, is presumed to have stolen them or, at least, to have known that the goods were stolen. Indeed sometimes a court will even refer to the operation of this so-called presumption as the "doctrine of recent possession". There is no presumption in such cases, much less a doctrine. What is permitted is an inference. A trier may, but is not obliged to, infer from the facts proved that the accused was the thief or knew of the goods' stolen character.[37] This is simply the operation of common sense as opposed to the operation of law. The prosecution on a charge of possession of stolen goods needs to prove that the accused was in possession of said goods and that the accused knew of their stolen nature. Suppose the prosecution leads evidence that the accused was found in possession of goods which were stolen 30 minutes earlier. The accused offered no explanation then or at

---

34 *Criminal Code*, s. 198(2).
35 See *R. v. Ortt*, [1969] 1 O.R. 461 at 463 (C.A.); *R. v. Steane*, [1947] 1 K.B. 997 at 1004; and *Hosegood v. Hosegood* (1950), 66 T.L.R. 735 at 738 (C.A.).
36 See, *e.g.*, *R. v. Oakes* (1986), 50 C.R. (3d) 1 (S.C.C.).
37 *R. v. Graham* (1972), 7 C.C.C. (2d) 93 (S.C.C.).

trial. The fact that the goods were recently stolen is circumstantial evidence from which it seems reasonable, an exercise in common sense, in the absence of any explanation forthcoming from the accused, to infer that the accused knew the goods were stolen.[38]

In the name of clarity of thought, presumptive language should be reserved for those evidentiary devices that mandate a result if the party against whom the presumption operates fails to either lead evidence to the contrary or fails to prove the contrary. The task assigned to the opponent varies depending on the language which created the presumption.

(b) True Presumptions

True presumptions mandate a finding, produce a legal consequence, but only if the opponent does not do as the legislation provides. Sometimes legislation will provide that the opponent has an evidential burden cast on him and failure to satisfy the same will demand that the trier find the presumed fact to exist. For example, the *Criminal Code* provides that it is an offence to break and enter a place with the intention of committing an indictable offence therein. The Code also provides that in the prosecution of such a case, where the prosecution leads evidence that the accused broke and entered, that, in the absence of evidence to the contrary, is proof of an intention to commit an indictable offence therein.[39] By the language of this statutory provision, "in the absence of any evidence to the contrary", there is an evidentiary burden cast on the accused. If there is no evidence indicating a contrary intention then the trier is mandated to conclude that there was an intention to commit an indictable offence in the place which was broken into. There is no may about it; it is a must.[40] In a civil case, our courts decided that a will was to be presumed to be made by a person with testamentary capacity. If there was evidence to the contrary, the effect of the presumption was lost and the proponent of the will would be obliged to prove testamentary capacity positively. This common law presumption cast an evidentiary burden on the opponent of the will.[41]

Sometimes the legislation creating a presumptive device will cast a persuasive burden on the accused. For example, the *Criminal Code* provides that in a prosecution for having the care or control of a motor vehicle while impaired, where it is proved that the accused occupied the seat ordinarily occupied by the driver, the trier will be obliged to find that the accused had

---

38 See *R. v. Kowlyk* (1988), 65 C.R. (3d) 97 (S.C.C.) extending the same common sense to the crime of break, enter and theft.

39 Section 348(2).

40 See *R. v. Proudlock* (1979), 5 C.R. (3d) 21 (S.C.C.).

41 *Robins v. National Trust,* [1927] A.C. 515 at 519; and *Smith v. Nevins,* [1925] S.C.R. 619 at 638.

care and control unless the accused establishes that he did not occupy the seat for the purpose of setting the vehicle in motion.[42] In such a case, even though the accused's testimony raised a reasonable doubt in the mind of the trier of fact as to whether the accused had care and control of the vehicle, the trier must convict if the accused did not satisfy his persuasive burden, failed to "establish", failed to persuade the trier to that effect.[43] When a persuasive burden is imposed on an accused in a criminal case, the burden is satisfied if the accused persuades the trier on a balance of probabilities; the accused never has to prove anything beyond a reasonable doubt.[44] In a civil case, our courts decided that there was a presumption of legitimacy for children born in lawful wedlock and the same was not to be displaced save by persuading the trier to the contrary.[45]

(c) **Presumptions and The Charter**

Section 1 1(d) of the Charter provides that any person charged with an offence has the right "to be presumed innocent until proven guilty according to law."[46]

In *Oakes*,[47] the accused had been charged with possession of a narcotic for the purpose of trafficking. The *Narcotic Control Act* provided that in such a prosecution the trial was to proceed as if it were a prosecution for simple possession. At the conclusion of the first stage, the Court was to make a finding as to whether the accused was in fact in possession. If the accused was found to be in possession, the Act provided that he was to be given the opportunity of establishing that he was not in possession for the purpose of trafficking. If the accused failed to establish this then he would be convicted of the much more serious offence of possession for the purpose of trafficking.[48] With respect to the proof of a material ingredient of the crime, the purpose of the possession, the accused, and not the prosecution, had the persuasive burden. All were in agreement that whenever a statutory provision placed a persuasive burden on an accused it would be satisfied by proof on a balance of probabilities and would not require proof beyond a reasonable doubt. The Court decided that the provision of the *Narcotic Control Act* was in violation of s. 11 (d) of the Charter. The Court announced the applicable test. If a provision cast a burden on the accused of disproving on a balance of probabilities an essential element of an offence, making a

---

42 Section 258.
43 *R. v. Appleby* (1971), 3 C.C.C. (2d) 354 (S.C.C.).
44 See *R. v. Oakes, supra,* note 36.
45 *Welstead v. Brown* (1951), [1952] 1 D.L.R. 465 (S.C.C.).
46 *Constitution Act, 1982,* R.S.C. 1985, App. II, No. 44.
47 *R. v. Oakes, supra,* note 36.
48 *Narcotic Control Act,* R.S.C. 1985, c. N-1, s. 8.

conviction possible despite the existence of a reasonable doubt concerning a material ingredient, that provision would be a violation of s. 11 (d) of the Charter. The Court later announced that there would be a violation whether the legislative provision had to do with an essential element, a collateral factor, an excuse or a defence; the characterization of the factor with respect to which the accused had a burden did not affect the analysis of the presumption of innocence.[49]

The Court then looked to s. 1 of the Charter to see whether this violation of the Charter could be justified. Section 1 of the Charter provides:

> The *Canadian Charter of Rights and Freedoms* guarantees the rights and freedoms set out in it subject only to such reasonable limits prescribed by law as can be demonstrably justified in a free and democratic society.

The violation in the *Oakes* case was prescribed by law, by s. 10 of the *Narcotic Control Act*. Therefore the violation could be considered under s. 1.

The Court announced what has become known as the "*Oakes* test" as the normal means for s. 1 analysis. First it is the party who seeks to uphold the provision under s. 1 who has the onus of proving that the provision is reasonable and demonstrably justified. The onus is on the balance of probabilities but the degree of probability will be high. There are two criteria that need to be satisfied. First, the objective, which the measures are designed to serve, must be of sufficient importance to warrant overriding a constitutionally protected right or freedom. The objective must, at a minimum, relate to concerns that are pressing and substantial. Care must be taken in this first step not to overstate the legislative objective. If the objective is stated too broadly, its importance may be exaggerated and the analysis compromised.[50] For example, in *Fisher*,[51] the accused was an employee of the government. He was charged under the *Criminal Code* with accepting a benefit without the written consent of the head of his branch. The Code cast a persuasive burden on the accused to prove he had the necessary consents.[52] The Crown, seeking to justify a violation of s. 11, argued that the objective of the impugned provision was the preservation of the integrity and the appearance of integrity of the public service. The Court decided this was too broad a description of the objective. It was the objective of the reverse onus clause contained in the section, rather than the objective of the whole of the section, which needed to be the focus of a s. t Charter analysis.

---

49 *R. v. Whyte* (1988), 64 C.R. (3d) 123 (S.C.C.).
50 *RJR-MacDonald Inc. v. Canada (Attorney General)* (1995), 100 C.C.C. (3d) 449 (S.C.C.), *per* McLachlin J.
51 *R. v. Fisher* (1994), 17 O.R. (3d) 295 (C.A.), leave to appeal to S.C.C. refused (1995), 35 C.R. (4th) 401 (S.C.C.).
52 Section 121(1)(b).

The reverse onus clause itself must have an underlying objective which is sufficiently important to warrant overriding s. 11 (d) of the Charter.

Second, the means chosen to achieve the objective must be seen to be proportional to the task. This second criterion has three components. First, the means chosen must be rationally connected to the objective. Second, the means chosen should impair the right or freedom as little as possible. This requirement is sometimes stated to be as little as possible but remaining as effective, but the courts have not been entirely consistent in this area.[53] Finally, there must be a proportionality between the effects of the measures which are responsible for limiting the right or freedom and the objective which has been identified as important.

In the result in the *Oakes* case, the Court decided that the provision there under review could not be saved by s. 1 as the provision was not internally rational. Possession of narcotics, regardless of amount, could not be said to rationally support an inference that the person was in possession for the purpose of trafficking. The Court refused to read limitations into the legislation to make it internally rational, though later courts have taken to reading into or reading down legislation to make it consistent with the Charter.[54]

It should be recognized that placing an evidential burden on the accused has also been seen to impair the accused's presumption of innocence.[55] For example, the *Criminal Code* provides that evidence that a person lives with a prostitute is, in the absence of evidence to the contrary, proof that the person lives on the avails of prostitution.[56] The language chosen for this presumptive device places an evidential burden on the accused. A conviction is mandated if there is no evidence to the contrary though there is no positive evidence as to the material ingredient of the offence that the accused actually did live on the avails. Our Court decided that this violated s. 11 (d) on the basis, per *Oakes,* that a conviction was mandated though there could be a

---

53 *R. v. Chaulk,* [1990] 3 S.C.R. 1303; and *R. v. Wholesale Travel Group Inc.,* [1991] 3 S.C.R. 154.

54 See, *e.g., R. v. Fisher, supra,* note 51, where the Court decided to delete the offensive words "the proof of which lies on him" and *R. v. Laba* (1994), 34 C.R. (4th) 360 (S.C.C.), where the Court redrafted the section to conform to the Charter. In *Laba,* the Court said there was no need for the provision to be internally rational; this statement is at odds with other Supreme Court decisions: see R. Delisle, "Confusion on Evidentiary Burdens" (1994), 34 C.R. (4th) 402. See also *R. v. Curtis* (1998), 14 C.R. (5th) 328 (Ont. C.A.) where the court simply deleted the offensive phrase "the proof of which lies upon him." Compare Delisle, *Stone: Judicial Activism Gone Awry to Presume Guilt,* (1999) 24 C.R. (5th) 91.

55 *R. v. Boyle* (1983), 5 C.C.C. (3d) 193 (Ont. C.A.); and *R. v. Downey* (1992), 13 C.R. (4th) 129 (S.C.C.).

56 Section 212(3).

reasonable doubt as to a material ingredient.[57] One might ask whether this guide, suitable when considering a statutory provision which imposes a persuasive burden, is also suitable when testing an evidential burden. If there was evidence led to the contrary the presumptive device would be spent and there would not be a conviction required. If there was no evidence led to the contrary, would it be possible for the trier to have a *reasonable* doubt?[58]

8. Judicial Notice

(a) Noticing Facts

We do not prove by evidence, indeed we cannot prove by evidence, all the facts that are necessary to a judicial decision. Certain matters are so well-known in the community or so easily ascertainable that a judge may be called on by a party to notice them.

Suppose a civil suit for damages sustained in a motor vehicle accident. The defendant describes his speed and his handling of the car. He maintains that the accident was unavoidable as he was unable to bring his vehicle to a stop in time to avoid the plaintiff's vehicle. The plaintiff maintains that the defendant was negligent in that he was driving too fast for the conditions of the road. The evidence indicates that it was raining at the time of the accident. To resolve the issue of negligence, do we need evidence that rain makes road surfaces wet, that the coefficient of friction between asphalt and tires is thereby reduced, that such fact is well-known to all drivers and that careful drivers lower their speed in such conditions? Such matters are so well-known in the community as to be indisputable. This material need not be proved in accordance with the normal rules of evidence. This knowledge is assumed to be already possessed by the judge and the party who has the burden of proof on the issue may simply call on the judge to judicially notice those facts which are necessary to the determination of the question.

The judge may not herself have the requisite knowledge and may need to be informed. Dictionaries, atlases and the like are ready to hand and may be freely consulted. In some cases she may even need to be informed by testimony concerning the matter; but in such cases the testimony is to inform the judge and the fact is decided, is noticed, by her and is not left open for a contrary decision by the jury. In *McQuaker v. Goddard*,[59] the plaintiff had been bitten by a camel at the defendant's zoo. In his suit for damages, the

---

57 *R. v. Downey, supra,* note 55.

58 See R. Delisle, "When Do Evidential Burdens Violate Section 11 (d)?" (1992), 13 C.R. (4th) 161.

59 [1940] 1 All E.R. 471 (C.A.).

plaintiff maintained that a camel is a wild animal and that, therefore, as a matter of substantive law, its owner was absolutely liable for any damage and there was no need for the plaintiff to show that the owner was aware of this particular animal's propensity to attack humans. The defendant called witnesses who testified that camels do not exist as wild anywhere in the world. This might appear to be evidence on an issue of fact and for the jury then to decide. But, and it's an important but, the decision in *McQuaker v. Goddard* was made by the judge. The judge took judicial notice of the ordinary course of nature, in this case the position of camels, and the evidence that was led was to assist him in that regard. The judge was then able to instruct the jury that they were to take it as a given that camels are domestic. The Court of Appeal upheld the trial judge's ruling that camels are domestic animals.

An interesting question arose in *Zundel*.[60] The accused was charged with publishing statements that he knew to be false and likely to cause mischief to the public interest. He had published a pamphlet "Did Six Million Really Die?" The Crown led witnesses who described the Holocaust. The Crown then asked the judge to judicially notice the fact of the Holocaust as notorious. The trial judge refused and the Court of Appeal agreed. The Court decided that to judicially notice the Holocaust would have necessitated the judge telling the jury that they must find the Holocaust to have occurred and this would have been prejudicial to the accused as it would have influenced the drawing of the inference concerning the accused's knowledge of the falsity of the pamphlet. The reader might ask whether taking judicial notice would have unfairly prejudiced the accused.[61]

Reported cases illustrate the sort of things that are commonly noticed by our judges dispensing with the need for formal proof. Our courts have decided, for example, that it is not necessary to prove that Victoria is in British Columbia,[62] that L.S.D. can be a mind destroying drugs,[63] that big horn sheep are mountain sheep,[64] or that "O.D.'d" means overdosed on a drug.[65]

While we see that in many instances the judicially noticed facts are indisputable, and the court whose attention is brought to them must notice them, there is also a discretion in the court for judicially noticing facts which are not demonstrated to be indisputable. This is a valid though delicate

60 *R. v. Zundel* (1987), 56 C.R. (3d) 1 (Ont. C.A.).

61 For criticism of the Court's approach see R. Delisle, Annotation to *Zundel* (1987), 56 C.R. (3d) 94.

62 *R. v. Kuhn* (1970), 1 C.C.C. (2d) 132 (B.C. Co. Ct.).

63 *R. v. Shaw* (1977), 36 C.R.N.S. 358 (Ont. C.A.).

64 *R. v. Quinn* (1976), 27 C.C.C. (2d) 543 (Alta. S.C.).

65 *R. v. MacAulay* (1975), 25 C.C.C. (2d) 1 (N.B. C.A.). See *R. v. Williams* (1998) 15 C.R. (5th) 227 (S.C.C.) where the Court sanctioned judicial notice of racism in the community.

exercise of judicial power. It requires as a matter of fairness to the parties that they be given notice of the judge's intention so that they might present information and argument as to its propriety.[66] It may be that there are respectable competing schools of thought as to whether the matter should be judicially noticed or proved by evidence in the normal way.[67]

There is a distinction, now commonly employed, between judicially noticing adjudicative facts and legislative facts.[68] Adjudicative facts are facts personal to the immediate parties before the court. They have to do with the what, where, when and how. Legislative facts are facts used by a court when it develops or creates law. Legislative facts are generally discovered by the judge from sources outside the avenues of formal proof and often in the absence of the parties. By their very nature, as the court is choosing which way the law should develop and make value judgments, legislative facts are seldom indisputable. Problems of fairness to the parties are generated by the silent use of legislative facts as the parties must frequently guess at the judge's appreciation of the applicable legislative facts and may not be given an opportunity to display contrary data to support a competing view.[69] With the advent of the *Charter of Rights and Freedoms,* and the task of determining the constitutionality of legislation, the courts are, of necessity, more frequently called on to judicially notice legislative facts.[70]

(b) Noticing Facts the Judge Personally Knows

It is one thing for a judge to judicially notice things which are generally known and another for a judge to notice things because the same has been proved before him in other cases. The latter is forbidden by our courts.[71] The adversary system dictates that the parties present the evidence and the trier should only notice things commonly known. If the judge has infor-

---

66 Compare *Moge v. Moge,* [1992] 3 S.C.R. 813 and *Cronk v. Canadian General Insurance Co.* (1995), 25 O.R. (3d) 505 (C.A.). See also *Daishowa Inc. v. Friends of the Lubicon* (1998), 39 O.R. (3d) 620 (Ont. Gen. Div.). Compare *R. v. Peter Paul* (1998), 18 C.R. (5th) 360 (N.B. C.A.), leave to appeal refused (1998), 204 N.B.R. (2d) 400 (note) (S.C.C.).

67 See Delisle, *The Dangers of Unrestricted Judicial Notice,* (1998) 12 C.R. (5th) 209.

68 Davis, "Judicial Notice" (1955), 55 Col. L. Rev. 945.

69 See *Moge* and *Cronk, supra,* note 66.

70 See, *e.g., R. v. Oakes, supra,* note 36, determining that drug trafficking was a sufficiently serious problem that one could see a legislative objective that was of sufficient importance to countenance a reverse onus provision violative of an accused's right to be presumed innocent. See *R. v. Hufsky* (1988), 63 C.R. (3d) 14 (S.C.C.) noticing the magnitude of the impaired driving problem in Canada and upholding as constitutional a violation of a person's right not to be arbitrarily detained.

71 *R. v. Holmes* (1923), 70 D.L.R. 851 (Alta. C.A.); *R. v. Dickson* (1973), 5 N.S.R. (2d) 240 (C.A.); and *R. v. Potts* (1982), 26 C.R. (3d) 252 (Ont. C.A.).

mation about the case before him, not shared by others, he should disregard the same or take the witness stand and be cross-examined as to whether his belief is accurate! Nevertheless, the line may be difficult to draw. For example, suppose an expert witness testifies before Judge A on Monday that it is not uncommon for a victim of sexual assault to recant an earlier complaint. Judge A takes that evidence into account in assessing the credibility of the complainant before him who did recant her accusation. Must he hear evidence again on Tuesday to similar effect? On Wednesday? Suppose he takes it into account and an appellate court decides he was right to take it into account.[72] At some point in time the evidence passes the stage of necessary testimony into the realm of judicial notice and from there into the domain of *stare decisis.*[73]

(c) Noticing Law

A judge is presumed to know the domestic law of the jurisdiction in which he presides -the domestic common and statutory law. If it is not ready to mind he is bound to acquire it. Information concerning the domestic law is not led by the parties through evidence though the parties may direct the judge to what they believe is the applicable law. There are some statutory provisions requiring the judge to notice federal and provincial legislation.[74] The judge is not restricted to information from the parties and, frequently, while having reserved his decision, he will inform himself as to the law. Should he be in error an appellate court is there to correct. If it is the final appellate tribunal discovering or creating the law we must accept its discovery as accurate. Delegated legislation is sometimes seen not to possess the requisite notoriety or accessibility for judicial notice and may need to be proved as a fact.[75]

---

72 *R. v. J. (F.E.)* (1990), 74 C.R. (3d) 269 (Ont. C.A.).

73 See *U.S. v. Lopez,* 328 F.Supp. 1077 (E.D.N.Y. 1971), *per* Weinstein J.

74 See, *e.g.,* the *Canada Evidence Act,* R.S.C. 1985, c. C-5, ss. 17 and 18. For provincial and territorial legislative provisions mandating judicial notice of statutes, see: R.S.A. 1980, c. A-18, s. 32; R.S.B.C. 1996, c. 124, s. 24; R.S.N.L. 1990, c. E-16, s. 26; R.S.M. 1997, c. E150, ss. 29 and 30; R.S.N.B. 1973, c. E-11, s. 70; R.S.N.L. 1990, c. E-16, s. 26; R.S.N.W.T. 1988, c. E-8, s. 38; R.S.N.S. 1989, c. 154, s. 3(3); R.S.O. 1990, c. I.11, s. 7; R.S.P.E.I. 1988, c. E-11, s. 21; R.S.S. 1978, c. S-16, s. 3(2); and R.S.Y. 1986, c. 57, s. 28.

75 See, for example, *R. v. Snelling,* [1952] O.W.N. 214 (H.C.). But compare *R. v. Smith,* [1988] O.J. No. 2551.

9. Real Evidence

(a) Generally

Aside from testimonial evidence, the trier might be informed by real evidence. Rather than having a witness describe the gun that was used, the gun itself might be placed into evidence. Rather than describing the intersection where the car accident occurred, the court may go to the scene and examine the intersection itself. The trier does not rely on what a witness has said; the trier becomes the witness. The kinds of real evidence are infinitely variable and here we will discuss some general principles applicable to all.

To be receivable, real evidence must, of course, be relevant and it will only be relevant to the matters in issue if the item offered into evidence is identified as genuine. The item must be authenticated to be what it is represented to be and the connection to the issues before the court made out. For example, in a prosecution for assault causing bodily harm, a blood stained shirt offered in evidence is not relevant to the matter in issue, that harm was visited on the victim, unless it is identified as having been worn by the victim on the evening in question. A witness must testify that this is the shirt. There are functions here for both the judge and the jury. The judge must be satisfied that there is sufficient evidence introduced to permit a rational finding by the jury that the item is as claimed. The jury will, later in their deliberations, weigh the evidence supposedly identifying the item, and will determine whether the item is in fact authentic.[76]

(b) Photographs

A picture, as we know, can be worth a thousand words. A photograph then is a common form of real evidence. The photograph may be a still photograph or a series of photos; in other words the same principles will be applicable to a still shot as are applicable to a videotape or a motion picture. In *Schaffner,*[77] the accused was charged with theft of moneys from the liquor store. He had been employed as a clerk. The management had noticed inordinately high shortages. They decided to use video surveillance. Attached to the video-cassette recorder were a time/date generator and a tape stacker. The generator imprinted directly on the videotape the date and the time. The stacker held three tapes, each of which provided four and a half hours of recording time and automatically ejected a recorded tape and inserted another tape in the machine. There was no operator present during the filming; the procedure was automatic. During the *voir dire,* the inves-

---

76 See, *e.g.*, *R. v. Parsons* (1977), 37 C.C.C. (2d) 497 (Ont. C.A.).
77 *R. v. Schaffner* (1988), 44 C.C.C. (3d) 507 (N.S. C.A.).

tigating officer showed and commented upon four tapes depicting irregularities on the part of the accused in conjunction with the detailed cash register tape for each particular day under study. He was able to properly identify the accused and pointed out four separate irregularities in the handling of cash by the accused. On appeal from conviction, the Court stated that a photograph is admissible in evidence if it accurately represents the facts, is not tendered with the intention to mislead and is verified on oath by a person capable to do so. This can be proved by anybody who is able to attest to those qualities. The photographer who took the pictures need not be called and there need not be an eye-witness to the matter recorded. In the result, the Court was satisfied that the tapes were properly authenticated and admitted into evidence.[78]

(c) Documents

The most common form of real evidence is a document. The authenticity of the tendered document may be established in a variety of ways. The party tendering may call the suggested writer, may call someone who saw the document being made, may have a witness compare the handwriting in the document with writing known by the witness to be that of the suggested writer,[79] may call experts in handwriting or experts in typefaces, and so on.

There are some documents so frequently encountered in litigation that the common law developed special rules of self-authentication. If a document is over 30 years old, there are no circumstances indicating fraud, and it is produced from a place where its custody would be natural, the circumstances call for it to be presumed authentic.[80] If a letter is received, purportedly signed by "Smith", the law will presume the letter to be authentic if it was received in response to an earlier letter addressed to Smith. The reply indicates knowledge in the signer which, relying on the habitual accuracy of the mails, could only have come from the earlier letter addressed to Smith.[81] The legislation is also filled with statutory provisions to aid in the authentication of government documents and judicial records.[82]

---

78 Compare *Clark v. O'Brien,* [1994] N.S.J. No. 586 with respect to "surprise" videos. Compare also *R. v. Nikolovski* (1996) 3 C.R. (5th) 362 (S.C.C.) with respect to a video where the victim cannot identify the accused but the trial judge can.

79 See, *e.g.,* s. 8 of the *Canada Evidence Act.* For similar provincial and territorial provisions, see: R.S.N.L. 1990, c. E-16, s. 25; R.S.N.W.T. 1988, c. E-8, s. 58; R.S.N.S. 1989, c. 154, s. 41; R.S.O. 1990, c. E.23, s. 57; and R.S.P.E.I. 1988, c. E-11, s. 20.

80 *Montgomery v. Graham* (1871), 31 U.C.Q.B. 57 (Ont. Q.B.).

81 See *Stevenson v. Dandy,* [1920] 2 W.W.R. 643 at 661 (Alta. C.A.).

82 See, *e.g., Canada Evidence,* ss. 19 to 23. For similar provincial and territorial provisions, see: R.S.A. 2000, c. A-18, ss. 27-31; R.S.B.C. 1996, c. 124, ss. 25-27; R.S.M. 1987, c. E150, ss. 34 and 38; R.S.N.B. 1975, c. E-11, ss. 25-34; R.S.N.L. 1990, c. E-16, ss. 20,

(d) The Best Evidence Rule

There was, before the detailed development of our rules of evidence, a broad rule at common law known as the best evidence rule. The rule had exclusionary and inclusionary aspects. If it was shown that there was better evidence available than that being tendered the tendered evidence would be rejected. If it was shown that the evidence being tendered was the very best available then it deserved receipt. As the rules of evidence developed, little remained of the rule and what does remain might better be called the documentary originals rule.[83] The documentary originals rule requires production of the original document unless the proponent of the evidence can satisfy the court that the original has been lost or destroyed or is in the possession of another and cannot be obtained. Also, certain statutory provisions have been enacted to provide for the introduction of copies when to produce the original would cause great inconvenience.[84]

The documentary originals rule was born at a time when copies of documents were made by hand and the possibility of error in the copying was real. Today, with modern photocopiers, insistence on the rule is often waived.[85]

(e) Views

If it is physically impossible to bring the real evidence into a courtroom, the courtroom may have to go to the evidence and take a view. There is statutory authority for the same.[86] Taking a view is disruptive of normal court proceedings and it will be up to the discretion of the trial judge who will assess the importance of the evidence against the disruption that will occur. The courts appear to be divided as to whether the view is only a device for better understanding the evidence adduced in the courtroom or whether the view is evidence in and of itself that may contradict evidence

---

21; R.S.N.W.T. 1988, c. E-8, ss. 31-40; R.S.N.S. 1989, c. 154, ss. 3-10; R.S.O. 1990, c. E.23, ss. 24-27; R.S.P.E.I. 1988, c. E-1 1, s. 22; R.S.S. 1978, c. S-16, ss. 3-9; and R.S.Y. 1986, c. 57, s. 29.

83 *Garton v. Hunter,* [1969] 1 All E.R. 451 at 453 (C.A.).

84 See, *e.g., Canada Evidence Act,* ss. 29 to 31. For similar provincial and territorial provisions, see: R.S.A. 1980, c. A-21, s. 34; R.S.B.C. 1996, c. 124, ss. 25-27; R.S.M. 1987, c. E-150, ss. 35-37; R.S.N.B. 1975, c. E-11, ss. 36-43; R.S.N. 1970, c. 115, ss. 20-26; R.S.N.W.T. 1988, c. E-8, ss. 39-49; R.S.N.S. 1989, c. 154, ss. 12-18; R.S.O. 1990, c. E.23, ss. 28-29; R.S.P.E.I. 1988, c. E-11, ss. 23-29; R.S.S. 1978, c. S-16, ss. 11-20; and R.S.Y. 1986, c. 57, ss. 30-35.

85 *R. v. Betterest Vinyl Manufacturing Ltd.* (1989), 52 C.C.C. (3d) 441 at 447-448 (B.C. C.A.).

86 See, *e.g.,* s. 652 of the *Criminal Code* and the *Ontario Rules of Civil Procedure,* R. 52.05.

given in the courtroom. The better position is the latter.[87] The former position confuses what is real evidence with what is sometimes referred to as demonstrative evidence. Demonstrative evidence, charts, models and the like are tools to assist the trier in understanding the evidence. Real evidence, whether tendered as an object within the courtroom or viewed outside is not a helpful aid but rather is evidence itself. Nevertheless, there is appellate authority to the contrary.[88]

---

87 See *Buckingham v. Daily News Ltd.,* [1956] 2 All E.R. 904 at 914 (C.A.), *per* Lord Denning; *Meyers v. Manitoba* (1960), 26 D.L.R. (2d) 550 (Man. C.A.); and *G & J Parking Lot Maintenance Ltd. v. Oland Construction Co.* (1978), 16 A.R. 293 (T.D.).

88 See *Chambers v. Murphy,* [1953] 2 D.L.R. 705 (Ont. C.A.); *Triple A Investments Ltd. v. Adams Brothers Ltd.* (1985), 56 Nfld. & P.E.I.R. 272 (Nfld. C.A.); and *Swadron v. North York (City)* (1985), 8 O.A.C. 204 (Div, Ct.).

3

Witnesses

1. Introduction

The testimonial qualifications of a witness are measured according to that witness's ability to observe, to recall her observation, and to accurately communicate her recollection to the trier of fact. The witness's ability to communicate has two aspects: the intellectual ability to understand questions and to give intelligent answers, and the moral responsibility to speak the truth. Each of these qualifications provides fertile ground for the cross-examiner to explore, for the benefit of the trier of fact, the credibility and hence the worth of the testimony offered in support of the proposition. Were you able to see? Do you now properly remember? What do you mean by those words? Do you hate my client? In the developmental years of the law of evidence the courts announced absolute prohibitions regarding some witnesses as they felt that the safeguard of cross-examination, for these witnesses, was not sufficient to the task of ensuring credibility. The deficiencies of these witnesses were seen as too large.

The early common law erected rules which completely forbade testimony from certain individuals who were regarded as incapable of exercising the normal powers of observation, recollection and communication. These individuals were ruled to be incompetent as witnesses. Later, the law refined its approach and decided that, rather than approaching these individuals as a class and rejecting them wholesale, it was preferable to examine the credentials of each particular individual being tendered as a witness. If the person was found to be competent, any deficiencies in testimonial qualifications would affect the weight to be given to their testimony rather than its admissibility.

Factors affecting competence could be organic, within the witness's own being, or emotional, as the result of a personal relationship with the matter being litigated or the parties thereto.

2. Organic Incapacity and the Oath

(a) Mental Illness

Initially a witness who was mentally ill was regarded as incompetent to take the witness stand. The courts came to recognize that this put the person who was mentally ill in a particularly vulnerable position. In *Hill*,[1] the accused was an attendant at a mental institution. He was charged with the manslaughter of one of the patients. The chief prosecution witness was another patient. It was objected that he was incompetent because of his mental illness. The precedents at the time were in conflict over whether there should be a blanket rule of inadmissibility. Instead of excluding him entirely the Court decided it would be better for the trial judge to conduct an examination of the particular individual whose mental capacity was questioned to determine whether the individual, though mentally ill, was nevertheless sufficiently aware of his moral responsibility to speak the truth in the courtroom and intellectually able to observe, recollect and communicate. There were seen to be two aspects to his competence: one moral and one intellectual. There were seen to be two possible sources of error: the witness might be unable to adequately appreciate the moral obligation of speaking the truth or the witness might not have the mental ability to accurately perceive and fully understand what he or she has seen or to properly remember or communicate the same. Although the witness in *Hill* had described his awareness of the consequences of a false oath — eternal damnation — the bulk of the evidence led on his testimonial qualifications concerned his ability to accurately observe, recollect and rationally communicate. Evidence was given that the witness did suffer the delusion that spirits spoke to him, but he was also described as having a good memory and a good ability to give an accurate account of events observed. It was decided that the trial judge was right in swearing the witness.

The common law is now embodied in statute:

16. (1) Where a proposed witness is a person . . . whose mental capacity is challenged, the court shall, before permitting the person to give evidence, conduct an inquiry to determine

(a) whether the person understands the nature of an oath or a solemn affirmation; and
(b) whether the person is able to communicate the evidence.

(2) A person referred to in subsection (1) who understands the nature of an oath or a solemn affirmation and is able to communicate the evidence shall testify under oath or solemn affirmation.

---

1 *R. v. Hill* (1851), 169 E.R. 495 (C.C.C.R.).

(3) A person referred to in subsection (1) who does not understand the nature of an oath or a solemn affirmation but is able to communicate the evidence may, notwithstanding any provision of any Act requiring an oath or a solemn affirmation, testify on promising to tell the truth.

(4) A person referred to in subsection (1) who neither understands the nature of an oath or a solemn affirmation nor is able to communicate the evidence shall not testify.

(5) A party who challenges the mental capacity of a proposed witness of fourteen years of age or more has the burden of satisfying the court that there is an issue as to the capacity of the proposed witness to testify under an oath or a solemn affirmation.[2]

Notice that the capacity of the adult witness is presumed. That capacity can be challenged and the challenger will have the onus of introducing sufficient evidence of incapacity. Then the party tendering the witness will have the burden of proving that the witness is competent.[3] The challenge regarding mental capacity should be taken at the outset and not after the witness has testified.[4] It would be wrong for counsel to sit in the bushes and wait to see whether the witness helps or hurts him. If the witness's incompetency only becomes manifest later the evidence might be stricken or the jury cautioned regarding its weight.[5] Notice that this *voir dire* should take place in the presence of the jury, the theory being that the jury will then be better able to evaluate the worth of what a witness has to say if he is allowed to speak.[6] The judge determines competence to speak and the jury determines credibility.

(b) Immaturity

The common law decided that children of tender years ought not to be regarded as incompetent to give evidence just because of their age. Rather, each was to be examined as an individual. Again if the case is tried by a jury the *voir dire* generally will be conducted in their presence so that the

---

2 *Canada Evidence Act,* R.S.C. 1985, c. C-5; as am. by R.S.C. 1985, c. 19 (3d Supp.), s. 18; S.C. 1994, c. 44, s. 89. Adopted by two provinces: see R.S.S. 1978, c. S-16, s. 42 and R.S.B.C. 1996, c. 124, s. 5.

3 *R. v. Hawke* (1975), 22 C.C.C. (2d) 19 at 27 (Ont. C.A.).

4 *R. v. Steinberg,* [1931] O.R. 222 at 257 (C.A.) and *R. v. Hawke, ibid.*

5 See the difficult case of *R. v. Thurlow* (1994), 34 C.R. (4th) 53 (Ont. Gen. Div.) where the court had to deal with a witness who admitted to having at least six different personalities.

6 See, *e.g., Toohey v. Metropolitan Police Commissioner,* [1965] 1 All E.R. 506 at 512 (H.L.): "[T]here would not be the inconvenience of having to exclude the jury, since the dispute would be for their use and their instruction." But see *R. v. Harbuz* (1979), 45 C.C.C. (2d) 65 (Sask. Q.B.).

jury will be better able to assess the worth of any testimony that is forth-coming.[7] However, the common law insisted that all testimony was to be on oath. Therefore the child would be examined to see whether the child possessed sufficient knowledge of the nature and consequences of an oath.[8] In this examination the trial judge would be interested in the child's intelligence and intellectual ability to observe, remember and communicate and also in the child's appreciation of the moral obligation to speak the truth.[9] Notice here that the child of tender years is presumed to be incompetent and competency needs to be established. Over the course of time, the judges fixed on the age of 14 as the age under which incompetency would be presumed and over which the child would be presumed competent. The age of 14 might have had something to do with the old *doli incapax* rule regarding criminal responsibility.

If the child was regarded as competent the child would be sworn and give her evidence. If the child was ruled incapable of taking an oath there was no way for her information to come before the court. In the nineteenth century the legislature recognized that children were at risk particularly with respect to sexual assault. Initially with respect to prosecutions for such assaults, and later expanded to all legal proceedings, the legislatures decided that a child, though ruled not competent to take an oath, could give evidence unsworn provided the child possessed sufficient intelligence to justify reception of the evidence and understood the duty of speaking the truth. Notice that this legislation laid down the rules for receiving unsworn evidence; the rules for receiving the sworn evidence of a child were laid down by the common law.

The *Canada Evidence Act* earlier provided:

> 16. (1) In any legal proceeding where a child of tender years is offered as a witness and the child does not, in the opinion of the judge, justice or other presiding officer, understand the nature of an oath, the evidence of the child may be received though not given upon oath, if, in the opinion of the judge, justice or other presiding officer, as the case may be, the child is possessed of sufficient intelligence to justify the reception of the evidence and understands the duty of speaking the truth.
>
> (2) No case shall be decided upon such evidence unless it is corroborated by some other material evidence.[10]

---

7   See generally *R. v. Ferguson* (1996), 112 C.C.C. (3d) 342 (B.C. C.A.).

8   *R. v. Brasier* (1779), 168 E.R. 202 (C.C.R.).

9   See, *e.g.*, *R. v. Horsburgh,* [1966] 1 O.R. 739 at 746 (CA.).

10   R.S.C. 1970, c. E-10. Using practically identical language, see provincial and territorial counterparts in R.S.A. 1980, c. A-21, s. 20; prior to 1992 amendments; R.S.N. 1970, c. 115, s. 15 A; R.S.N.W.T. 1988, c. E-8, ss. 19 and 25; R.S.N.S. 1989, c. 154, s. 63; prior to 1995 amendments; and R.S.Y. 1986, c. 57, ss. 16 and 22.

The tests for giving sworn evidence and unsworn evidence appear to be very similar. Initially the difference lay in the nature of the oath. To be sworn the child needed to recognize that she was calling on God to witness her evidence; taking an oath was the solemn assumption before God of an obligation to tell the truth.[11] More recently, the courts have decided that an awareness of God is not essential and that to be sworn the child needs only to appreciate the solemnity of the occasion and the added responsibility to tell the truth involved in taking an oath over and above the duty to tell the truth which is an ordinary duty of normal social conduct.[12]

Notice that the legislation provided that if the evidence of the child was given unsworn the matter could not be decided on such evidence alone but rather it was necessary that the evidence be corroborated by some other material evidence. Notice that this is a mandatory requirement of corroboration applicable by legislation to both civil and criminal cases. It is not a piece of advice to the jury to be cautious but rather a rule of law that you cannot convict on such evidence, even if you are satisfied beyond a reasonable doubt and you cannot decide a civil matter even if you're persuaded by the evidence to a balance of probabilities. Corroboration requires additional evidence, independent of the witness, which confirms the witness's evidence. In criminal cases, it must implicate the accused in a material way.

Recently, the federal Legislature has amended its legislation. The *Canada Evidence Act* now provides:

16. (1) Where a proposed witness is a person under fourteen years of age . . . the court shall, before permitting the person to give evidence, conduct an inquiry to determine

(a) whether the person understands the nature of an oath or a solemn affirmation; and
(b) whether the person is able to communicate the evidence.

(2) A person referred to in subsection (1) who understands the nature of an oath or a solemn affirmation and is able to communicate the evidence shall testify under oath or solemn affirmation.

(3) A person referred to in subsection (1) who does not understand the nature of an oath or a solemn affirmation but is able to communicate the evidence may, notwithstanding any provision of any Act requiring an oath or a solemn affirmation, testify on promising to tell the truth.

---

11 *R. v. Bannerman* (1966), 55 W.W.R. 257 (Man. C.A.); and *R. v. Budin* (1981), 58 C.C.C. (2d) 352 at 355 (Ont. C.A.).
12 *R. v. Fletcher* (1982), 1 C.C.C. (3d) 370 (Ont. C.A.), and *R. v. Khan* (1990), 59 C.C.C. (3d) 92 (S.C.C.).

(4) A person referred to in subsection (1) who neither understands the nature of an oath or a solemn affirmation nor is able to communicate the evidence shall not testify.

(5) A party who challenges the mental capacity of a proposed witness of fourteen years of age or more has the burden of satisfying the court that there is an issue as to the capacity of the proposed witness to testify under an oath or a solemn affirmation.[13]

It is now provided that where a proposed witness is a person under the age of 14 the court is to determine whether the person understands the nature of an oath or a solemn affirmation and whether the person is able to communicate the evidence. Notice again that there are two things being required: moral and intellectual capacity. Being able to communicate the evidence means being able to perceive and interpret the events in question and to recollect accurately and communicate them at trial.[14] Communicate does not mean only that the witness is able to understand the questions put and able to intelligently respond; the trial judge must be satisfied that the witness has the capacity to perceive, interpret and recollect along with the ability to intelligently articulate answers to questions. This capacity is to be tested by questions of a general nature and not by questions as to the events in issue. If the court decides the person has both of these capacities, the witness will testify under oath or solemn affirmation. If the court decides that the person does not understand the nature of an oath or solemn affirmation but is able to communicate, the person may give his or her evidence on promising to tell the truth. The court needs to inquire whether the witness understands what it means to promise to tell the truth. Does the witness understand the duty to speak the truth? A witness who can communicate the evidence should be allowed to testify under s. 16(3) only if he or she understands the duty to speak the truth in terms of everyday social conduct.[15]

The statute says that "the court shall . . . conduct an inquiry". Normally it is the judge who asks the questions of the child but there is now a recognition that the Crown, who is less of a stranger to the child, may be the better questioner. Just because the court is to conduct the inquiry does not necessarily mean that the court must actually ask the questions.[16] There is also authority that counsel who is calling the child should instruct the

---

13   Adopted by some provinces: see R.S.B.C. 1996, c. 124, s. 5; R.S.M. 1987, c. E150, s. 24 (as am. s.m. 1992, c. 15, s. 3); R.S.N.L. 1990, c. E-16, ss. 18, 18.1 and R.S.S. 1978 c. S-16, s. 42. For recent changes in Ontario, going even further, see the Ontario *Evidence Act*, R.S.O. 1990, c. E.23 ss. 18-18.2 (as am. S.O. 1995, c. 6, s. 6).

14   *R. v. Marquard* (1993), 25 C.R. (4th) 1 (S.C.C.).

15   *R. v. Farley* (1995), 40 C.R. (4th) 190 (Ont. C.A.).

16   *R. v. Peterson* (1996), [1996] O.J. No. 714, 1996 CarswellOnt 628 (C.A.), leave to appeal refused [1996] 3 S.C.R. xii; and *R. v. Caron* (1994), 94 C.C.C. (3d) 466 (Ont. C.A.).

child as to the nature of the inquiry he or she will have to undergo.[17] It is manifestly unfair to the witness to fail in this obligation.

There is no statutory requirement of corroboration in this new legislation. Judicial decisions, however, have expressed concerns, and often require instructions, depending on the facts of the particular case, as to the weight to be given to a child's evidence,[18] even if sworn.[19] A child's evidence is to be treated with caution where such caution is merited in the circumstances of the case. It is wrong to apply negative stereotypes to the evidence of children generally but rather each child should be approached as an individual. Our courts have said that while we cannot expect child witnesses to perform in the same manner as adults, this does not mean that the courts should subject their testimony to a lower level of scrutiny for reliability. It would be wrong to adopt an undiscriminating acceptance of the evidence of children while holding adults to higher standards. If the child gives his or her evidence unsworn, on a promise to tell the truth, the jury is to be reminded of that and cautioned.[20]

3. The Oath and The Affirmation

At common law, it was decided fairly early on that anyone could take an oath provided they believed in a God and future rewards and punishments. The oath need not be a Christian oath.[21] The form of the oath is not prescribed by law. Nothing is said about its form in the *Canada Evidence Act*. The Ontario *Evidence Act* does provide a form of oath involving kissing the Old or New Testament but also provides that should the witness object to such form any form may be followed that binds his conscience.[22] By definition, an "oath" is calling on God to witness that a person is going to tell the truth and involves a recognition that God will either reward him or

---

17 *R. v. Bannerman, supra,* note 11.

18 See, *e.g., R. v. S. (W.)* (1994), 29 C.R. (4th) 143 (Ont. C.A.), leave to appeal to S.C.C. refused (1994), 35 C.R. (4th) 402 (note) (S.C.C.); *R. v. Marquard, supra,* note 14; *R. v. K. (V.)* (1991), 4 C.R. (4th) 338 at 357 (B.C. C.A.); *R. v. J. (F.E.)* (1990), 74 C.R. (3d) 269 (Ont. C.A.); *R. v. W. (R.)* (1992), 74 C.C.C. (3d) 134 (S.C.C.), application for re-hearing refused (November 18, 1992), Doc. 21820 (S.C.C.); and *R. v. W. (R.S.)* (1992), 74 C.C.C. (3d) 1 at 8 (Man. C.A.).

19 See *R. v. Horsburgh, supra,* note 9.

20 *R. v. Marquard, supra,* note 14.

21 *Omychund v. Barker* (1744), 26 E.R. 15 (C.A.).

22 R.S.O. 1990, c. E.23, s. 16. To like effect, see R.S.M. 1987, c. E.150, ss. 14 and 15; R.S.N.B. 1973, c. E-11, s. 13; R.S.N.W.T. 1988, c. E-8, s. 23; on a bible or with uplifted hand: R.S.A. 1980, c. A-21, ss. 16 and 17; oath with an uplifted hand: R.S.B.C. 1996, c. 124, s. 22. No form prescribed in Saskatchewan, Nova Scotia, Newfoundland, the Yukon Territory or Prince Edward Island.

punish him in this world or the next. Our courts have said, however, that though this is not present, a witness, child or adult, may take an oath if he understands the added responsibility of telling the truth in the courtroom. In *Fletcher*,[23] the Court recognized that as society has changed over the years the oath for many has lost its spiritual and religious significance. Nonetheless, the sense of moral obligation, that his conscience will be bound by it, will suffice for the adult to take an oath.

Some people who did believe in God were excluded as witnesses. For example, the Quakers thought it wrong to call on God to witness their temporal matters. Legislation was enacted to accommodate them. The *Canada Evidence Act* provides:

> 14. (1) A person may, instead of taking an oath, make the following solemn affirmation:
>
> I solemnly affirm that the evidence to be given by me shall be the truth, the whole truth and nothing but the truth.
>
> (2) Where a person makes a solemn affirmation in accordance with subsection (1), his evidence shall be taken and have the same effect as if taken under oath.

As an example of provincial legislation, the Ontario *Evidence Act* provides:

> 17.—(1) Where a person objects to being sworn from conscientious scruples, or on the ground of his or her religious belief, or on the ground that the taking of an oath would have no binding effect on the person's conscience, he or she may, in lieu of taking an oath, make an affirmation or declaration that is of the same force and effect as if the person had taken an oath in the usual form.[24]

Again it seems sensible for counsel calling a witness to advise that witness, in advance of the proceedings, of his options. Indeed it is sensible for counsel, knowing her witness's preferences, to announce the same to the court as the witness proceeds to the stand so that the witness does not himself have to take on that obligation. The witness is normally strange to the setting and may find it difficult to announce his preference in a crowded courtroom.

---

23 *R. v. Fletcher, supra,* note 12.
24 For similar provisions in other provinces, see: R.S.A. 2000, c. A-18, s. 17; R.S.B.C. 1996, c. 124, s. 20; R.S.M. 1987, c. E150, s. 16; R.S.N.B. 1973, c. E-11, s. 14; R.S.N.W.T. 1988, c. E-8, s. 21; R.S.N.S. 1989, c. 154, s. 62; R.S.P.E.I. 1988, c. E-11, s. 13; R.S.S. 1978, c. S-16, s. 46; and R.S.Y. 1986, c. 57, s. 20.

4. Emotional Incapacity

At common law, persons who were seen to be interested in the outcome of a piece of litigation were regarded as incompetent to be witnesses. A rather blunt tool to be sure but the law decided that such persons were so suspect that they should not be heard at all. This disqualification therefore meant that the parties to a matter, the plaintiff and the defendant in a civil trial, and the accused in a criminal trial, were not competent as witnesses. The law also saw the spouses of the parties to be similarly interested and spouses as well were regarded as incompetent.

There was one exception regarding spouses. The law early recognized that a spouse was vulnerable to abuse that might never be prosecuted if the spouse was incompetent to speak and therefore the common law provided that a spouse could testify against her spouse if she was the subject of his abuse.[25] This exception was preserved by legislation.[26] In fact, it has since been decided that in such a case the spouse is also a compellable witness at the instance of the prosecution.[27] Our courts have reasoned that in a case of spousal abuse it is not just the spouse who is interested in a successful prosecution — society also has an interest. Such crimes are common, the consequences frequently grave and, since these crimes are usually committed in the privacy of the home, they are often impossible to prosecute unless the victim testifies.

Reforming legislation came about in the nineteenth century. Parties and their spouses were rendered competent as witnesses and their interest was left to impact solely on the weight to be given to their testimony. For example, the Ontario *Evidence Act* provides:

> 8.—(1) The parties to an action and the persons on whose behalf it is brought, instituted, opposed or defended are, except as hereinafter otherwise provided, competent and compellable to give evidence on behalf of themselves or of any of the parties, and the husbands and wives of such parties and persons are, except as hereinafter otherwise provided, competent and compellable to give evidence on behalf of any of the parties.[28]

The *Canada Evidence Act* provides, however, that in a criminal prosecution the accused and his spouse are competent witnesses only for the defence:

---

25   See *Lord Audley's Trial* (1631), 3 Howell's State Trials 401 (H.L.).
26   Section 4(6) of the *Canada Evidence Act*.
27   *R. v. McGinty* (1986), 52 C.R. (3d) 161 (Y.T. C.A.), approved in *Salituro, infra,* note 30.
28   See also R.S.A. 2000, c. A-18, s. 4; R.S.B.C. 1996, c. 124, s. 7; R.S.M. 1987, c. E150, s. 4; R.S.N.B. 1973, c. E-11, s. 3; R.S.N.L. 1990, c. E-16, s. 2; R.S.N.W.T. 1988, c. E-8, s. 3; R.S.N.S. 1989, c. 154, s. 45; R.S.P.E.I. 1988, c. E-11, ss. 2, 3 and 4; R.S.S. 1978, c. S-16, ss. 34 and 35; and R.S.Y. 1986, c. 57, s. 3.

4. (1) Every person charged with an offence, and, except as otherwise provided in this section, the wife or husband, as the case may be, of the person so charged, is a competent witness for the defence, whether the person so charged is charged solely or jointly with any other person.[29]

The accused in a criminal case cannot therefore be called as a witness by the prosecution. Whether he takes the witness stand is solely up to him. This lack of general competence in the accused is rooted in the privilege against self-incrimination. The spouse's lack of competence was evidently rooted in the notion that it was wrong for the courts to disrupt marital harmony by having a spouse testify against the interests of the other. Recognizing this as the basis for their lack of competence our courts have recently decided that where there is no marital harmony to disrupt, where the spouses though married are irreconcilably separated, a spouse may testify.[30] The federal legislation also provides for a spouse's competence and compellability with respect to certain crimes, largely sexual offences,[31] and with respect to some crimes where the victim is under the age of 14 years.[32]

5. Manner of Questioning

The principal source of information at a trial is oral testimony elicited out of the mouths of witnesses called by the parties. The fact that the witnesses were chosen by the parties, and that they may have been prepared by the parties as to how to give their evidence, led to different rules regarding the manner of questioning depending on who puts the questions.

The witness's description of the incident under review is first elicited by the party who called him. This process is called examination-in-chief or direct examination. At the conclusion of the direct examination, the adversary is allowed to ask questions of the witness. The adversary is then able to elicit other data concerning the incident which might be favourable to his position. The adversary is also able to put questions to the witness concerning his powers of perception and memory, to demand explicitness in his

---

29 In *R. v. Gosselin* (1903), 33 S.C.R. 255 (S.C.C.), the Court interpreted "competent" in the predecessor to s. 4(1) as competent and compellable. The legislation at that time did not contain the words "for the defence" following "competent". Those words, perhaps in response to *Gosselin,* were added in 1906 (S.C. 1906, 6 Edw. V11, c. 10). In *R. v. Amway Corp.,* [1989] 1 S.C.R. 21, Sopinka J., for the Court, said that it was apparent from the words of s. 4(1) that "it addresses only one of the two components of the rights and obligations of a witness: that is, competence. It does not purport to deal with compellability."

30 *R. v. Salituro,* [1991] 3 S.C.R. 654.

31 Section 4(2) of the *Canada Evidence Act.*

32 Section 4(3) of the *Canada Evidence Act.*

communication and to explore his sincerity. These questions are designed to challenge the accuracy of the witness's description of the incident. This process is known as cross-examination. Notice that there are two purposes in cross-examining: to gain additional information from the witness that the adversary neglected to bring out and to attack the worth of the evidence that was elicited. After cross-examination, the witness may be re-examined by the party who called him and the witness will be given an opportunity to explain or amplify answers given on cross-examination. Further opportunities to cross-examine and re-examine, all at the discretion of the trial judge, are possible.

(a) Leading Questions

Speaking generally, we say that the party who calls a witness should not ask the witness leading questions. A leading question is one which suggests the answer. The reason for the prohibition is obvious. There is a concern that since the party has chosen to call this witness, this witness favours that party and will readily agree to any suggestions put in the form of questions. This concern is amplified by the fact that counsel will have gone over the witness's evidence in advance of the trial and the witness will understand what answers are preferable. The trier of fact deserves the evidence of the witness as opposed to the evidence of the lawyer who is putting the questions and therefore suggestive questions must be avoided.

Like all rules of evidence this rule should not be applied if the reason for the rule does not exist. In determining whether a question suggests an answer, much will depend on the character, mood and bias of the witness, and the manner and inflection of the questioner, all matters particularly suited to the exercise of discretion by the trial judge. If the matter being pursued is a preliminary matter, such as identifying the witness and his means of knowledge, leading questions are not only permitted but are also the sign of a good advocate who has chosen not to waste the time of the court. If it is necessary to identify for the witness the particular matter that the examiner wishes to explore, leading questions may be necessary and are therefore permitted. If it is seen to be necessary to refresh the witness's memory or if there is an apparent problem with the witness due to age, education, language or mental capacity, the trial judge will relax the rule and permit leading questions as the reason for the prohibition will be seen to not exist. Finally, if the witness appears to all and sundry to be clearly hostile to the examiner's position, clearly not ready to adopt any suggestion of the questioner, the examiner will ask the trial judge for a declaration of hostility and then leading questions will be permitted.

From the above it may be deduced that while, generally speaking, leading questions are prohibited when counsel is examining in chief, leading questions are permitted in cross-examination. Indeed, leading questions are the hallmark of cross-examination. That's what distinguishes cross from direct. Cross-examination is not asking all the same questions that were asked in chief but asking them in a cross manner although as carried out by some advocates it might appear to be so.

Also from the above analysis it might appear logical that if it appears to the trial judge that the witness being cross-examined actually favours the position of the cross-examiner, the trial judge should have the power to restrain the questioner. Again we want the evidence of the witness and not the evidence of the questioner. Although apparently logical, our law says there is no such power. Rather, the weight to be given to the answers in such a situation will be affected.[33]

Apart from leading questions, there is also a prohibition against what might be called misleading questions. It is wrong for counsel to phrase a question so as to assume within it the truth of some fact which remains controverted between the parties as the witness may be unfairly misled. The classic example is "When did you stop beating your wife?"

(b) Refreshing Memory

The following deals with the refreshment of a witness's memory while the witness is in the stand. While there are, of course, ethical considerations which forbid placing a story in the mouth of a prospective witness, there does not appear to be any restrictions on the methods used for such a purpose prior to the trial.[34] If, however, the witness refreshed his memory from his notes just before coming to court, the opposing counsel should have the opportunity to see the same for the purpose of possible impeachment. In *Monfils*,[35] during cross-examination at a preliminary hearing, a police constable testified that prior to his appearance in Court he had refreshed his memory by reading his entire notes. He agreed that there was in his notes a particular utterance which he had testified had been made by one of the accused and counsel for the defence asked for the production of the officer's notes. The Provincial Court judge ruled that the notes were to be produced and on appeal he was upheld. This seems sensible as it should not matter

---

33 See, *e.g.*, *R. v. McLaughlin* (1974), 2 O.R. (2d) 514 (C.A.).

34 See, *e.g.*, *R. v. Allen (No. 2)* (1979), 46 C.C.C. (2d) 477 (Ont. H.C.) re the use of sodium amytol, and *Kowall v. McRae,* [1980] 2 W.W.R. 492 (Man. C.A.) re the use of hypnosis. See *Reference re R. v. Coffin,* [1956] S.C.R. 191, where the Supreme Court sanctioned the use by a witness, prior to going into the stand, of the transcript of the witness's evidence given at the preliminary.

35 *R. v. Monfils,* [1972] 1 O.R. 11 at 11-13 (C.A.).

whether the notes were used just before coming to court or later while in the confines of the court.[36]

A witness in the stand may profess a lack of memory concerning the incident. That witness may then be shown notes concerning the incident made at an earlier time and, on seeing the notes, two things are possible. The witness, on seeing the notes, might profess a present memory concerning the matter. We have all had the experience of failing to remember a matter but on being reminded of something associated with the matter having the memory released thereby. The triggering device might be a note, a song, or a picture. In most cases that concern us, the trigger will be a note. In such a case, we have a true case of refreshment of memory and the witness will be permitted to testify, in accordance with that memory, concerning the event. We employ a piece of jargon and say that this is a case of present memory revived. On the other hand, on seeing the notes the witness might say that the notes do not revive his memory concerning the incident but that he remembers making the notes, remembers that the notes were made contemporaneously with the incident or at a time shortly thereafter when the events were fresh in his mind, and that the notes accurately record the incident. The witness who now has no present memory of the matter is prepared to vouch for the accuracy of the earlier description. In this situation, the so-called refreshment of memory is actually a case of past recollection recorded.[37]

Both phenomena, although distinct in their nature, are generally referred to as under the umbrella of refreshing the memory of the witness. This is unfortunate. In a case of past recollection recorded it is the earlier note that is speaking. The earlier out-of-court statement is received as evidence of its truth, under the guise of refreshing memory, as an exception to the hearsay rule.[38] In this instance it is the out-of-court statement that is the evidence and deserves to be received.[39] To guarantee reliability we insist that the statement be one made by the witness at the time of the incident. Those requirements are appropriate in a case of past recollection recorded. They operate to ensure accuracy of recording and of memory. The adversary is unable to test the witness's present memory in cross-examination and there needs to be other assurances. If, on the other hand, we have a true case of the memory being refreshed, the evidence is the testimony of the witness and not the note earlier made. The witness is thereby open for cross-examination as to whether he actually does have a present memory and to be

---

36 But see *R. v. Kerenko* (1964), [1965] 3 C.C.C. 52 (Man. C.A.).
37 These phrases were coined by Professor Wigmore: see 3 Wigmore, *Evidence* (Chad. Rev.), s. 735.
38 See *R. v. Meddoui* (1991), 61 C.C.C. (3d) 345 (Alta. C.A.).
39 See the review in *R. v. Green* (1994), 32 C.R. (4th) 248 (Ont. Gen. Div.).

questioned regarding the accuracy of his present memory. This is not a case of hearsay. The requirements of contemporaneity and that the notes be made by the witness deserve, in such a situation, to be relaxed.[40]

When a witness uses notes to refresh memory the adversary is also entitled to look at the notes and to ask questions of the witness concerning them. Were the notes made by the witness himself or were they made in collaboration with others? Why are there seeming interlineations? Erasures? What of the other notes which seem to qualify the witness's evidence?

(c) Examination by the Court and the Order of Witnesses

In a civil case, the court has no power to call witnesses. Who will be called as a witness is a decision for the parties.[41] The court may call a witness in a criminal case when it is seen to be in the interests of justice.[42] In criminal cases, society has its own interest in gaining the truth. In civil trials, while truth is important, justice in the sense that both litigants feel satisfied that their dispute, framed and processed by them, was properly settled, is paramount.

The prosecution is not entitled to split its case and therefore cannot call further witnesses after the defence has closed its case unless the matter has arisen *ex improviso, i.e.,* a matter which human ingenuity could not have foreseen.[43] This limitation is also applicable to the judge who may not call witnesses after the defence has closed its case.[44]

Both in civil and in criminal cases, the court has the right to ask questions of the witnesses to clarify matters. In exercising this right the court should be cautious as it does not know as much about the case as the parties and interference can have the opposite effect to that intended.[45]

---

40 See *R. v. Bengert (No. 5)*, [1979] 1 W.W.R. 472 (B.C. S.C.), affirmed (*sub nom. R. v. Bengert (No. 11)*) (1980), 53 C.C.C. (2d) 481 at 522 (B.C. C.A.). For recent decisions dealing with refreshing memory see generally *R. v. Shergill* (1997), 13 C.R. (5th) 160 (Ont. Gen. Div.), *R. v. B. (K.G.)* (1998), 125 C.C.C. (3d) 61 (Ont. C.A.) and *R. v. Mattis* (1998), 20 C.R. (5th) 93 (Ont. Prov. Div.).

41 See *Re Fraser* (1912), 26 O.L.R. 508 at 521 (C.A.); and *Fowler v. Fowler*, [1949] O.W.N. 521 (C.A.).

42 See *R. v. Brouillard*, [1985] 1 S.C.R. 39 at 44; and *R. v. MacPhee* (1985), 19 C.C.C. (3d) 345 (Alta. Q.B.).

43 See *R. v. John* (1985), 49 C.R. (3d) 57 (S.C.C.). This limitation also exists with respect to a judge's right to call a witness: see *R. v. MacPhee, ibid.* With respect to proper rebuttal, see *R. v. Wood* (1986), 28 C.C.C. (3d) 65 (Ont. C.A.).

44 *R. v. Morin* (1977), 40 C.R.N.S. 378 (Sask. Dist. Ct.).

45 See *Jones v. National Coal Board,* [1957] 2 Q.B. 55 at 63 (C.A.); and *R. v. Rhodes* (1981), 59 C.C.C. (2d) 426 (B.C. C.A.).

While the judge in criminal cases has no control over the order in which the accused calls his witnesses,[46] many provinces have enacted in rules of court governing civil cases a power in the court to require that the party be examined before other witnesses on his behalf.[47] These rules also provide power in the court to order the exclusion of prospective witnesses until they are required to give evidence. In criminal cases, there is inherent power in the court, to ensure a fair trial, to order the exclusion of witnesses. Since the accused has the right to be present during the whole of his trial he cannot be the subject of such an order. At one time it was understood that if an accused was going to testify he should testify first. That is no longer a requirement but if he does not testify first and so gains the advantage of listening to his witnesses being examined and cross-examined before himself going into the witness box, he risks a comment being made as to his credibility.[48]

6. Impeachment of a Witness

Aside from weakening a witness's description of a matter by cross-examination, the adversary is permitted to impeach the credibility of a witness by other evidence. This may be done by showing that the witness on another occasion made a statement concerning the matter which is inconsistent with her present testimony, by evidencing a bias in the witness which would cause the witness to be inaccurate, by extrinsic evidence attacking the character of the witness, or by leading evidence attacking the capacity of the witness to observe, remember or communicate.

(a) Prior Inconsistent Statements

A trier of fact is entitled to accept all, part or none of a witness's evidence. Contradiction on one aspect of the testimony will be taken into account when assessing the credibility of the witness in other aspects; if the witness is seen to be in error on one point, he is seen to be at least capable of error on other points. If counsel can establish that the witness on another occasion made a statement which is inconsistent with his present testimony he has displayed a capacity to err as both statements cannot be correct. He might then ask the witness "When were you lying? Then or now?"

---

46 *R. v. Smuk* (1971), 3 C.C.C. (2d) 457 (B.C. C.A.); and *R. v. Angelantoni* (1975), 31 C.R.N.S. 342 (Ont. C.A.).
47 See, *e.g.,* Ontario Rule 52.06(2).
48 But see R. v. P. (T.L.) (1996), 193 A.R. 146 (Alta. C.A.).

(b) Collateral Facts Limitation

Counsel may be able to elicit the earlier inconsistent statement out of the mouth of the witness during cross-examination. If the witness does not admit making an earlier statement inconsistent with his present testimony counsel may have to independently prove the same. If that method of contradiction proved necessary the common law developed a limitation.

The common law was concerned that independent proof of a previous inconsistent statement carried with it certain problems. First, there was the amount of time to be taken in such an exercise. Second, there was concern that the trier of fact could be led away from the main issue before it and become confused. Third, it was seen to be unfair to a witness who came to court to testify concerning a particular matter to be confronted with inconsistencies about other matters. The common law came up with a rule called the collateral facts rule. It is simple to state: while a witness may be asked all manner of questions impacting on credibility he may not be contradicted by independent proof if the matter is collateral. If the matter is collateral the cross-examiner must accept the answer given.

While the rule is easy to articulate, the determination of exactly what is collateral has proved to be difficult. Some would ask whether the matter would be independently provable whether or not the question was put on cross-examination. If the answer is yes then the matter is not collateral. If independently provable the matter has relevance to the material issues being litigated or to a testimonial factor affecting the witness and is therefore not collateral. A variant on this would be to ask whether the matter had meaning apart from the contradiction *simpliciter*. If yes, then the matter is not collateral. If the evidence shows that the witness has a bias against the cross-examiner's party then, that matter going to the capacity of the witness to accurately describe the matters in issue, the evidence is not collateral.

The wisest approach might be to define collateral in terms of the reason for the rule. If the matter was seen as having great probative value either regarding the material issues or the credibility of the witness, if the introduction of the evidence would not confuse or mislead the trier, if proof would not consume too much time, and if it would not be unfair to the witness then the matter should not be regarded as collateral. In other words, if the matter is important it's not collateral. If it's unimportant it's collateral.[49]

The legislatures have now enacted a procedure for impeaching a witness by a previous inconsistent statement. For example, the *Canada Evidence Act* provides:

---

49 See Younger, *The Art of Cross-Examination* (1974) ABA Monograph Series at 15.

10. (1) On any trial a witness may be cross-examined as to previous statements that the witness made in writing, or that have been reduced to writing, or recorded on audio tape or video tape or otherwise, relative to the subject-matter of the case, without the writing being shown to the witness or the witness being given the opportunity to listen to the audio tape or view the video tape or otherwise take cognizance of the statements, but, if it is intended to contradict the witness, the witness' attention must, before the contradictory proof can be given, be called to those parts of the statement that are to be used for the purpose of so contradicting the witness, and the judge, at any time during the trial, may require the production of the writing or tape or other medium for inspection, and thereupon make such use of it for the purposes of the trial as the judge thinks fit.

. . .

11. Where a witness, on cross-examination as to a former statement made by him relative to the subject-matter of the case and inconsistent with his present testimony, does not distinctly admit that he did make the statement, proof may be given that he did in fact make it, but before that proof can be given the circumstances of the supposed statement, sufficient to designate the particular occasion, shall be mentioned to the witness, and he shall be asked whether or not he did make the statement.[50]

Section 10 has to do with written statements and s. 11 with oral. The legislation incorporates the common law collateral facts rule by saying the earlier statement has to be "relative to the subject-matter of the case". The statute provides that counsel in cross-examination is allowed to ask questions concerning the earlier statement, and if in writing without first showing the witness the statement, but that if he is intended to independently prove the statement the witness must first be reminded of the circumstances of the earlier statement and how it is suggested that there is a contradiction. This provides the witness the opportunity to explain or accept the earlier statement. This process is economical since if the witness accepts that he did make the earlier statement it obviates the need for independent proof. It is also a case of simply being fair to the witness and allowing him to offer, if he can, an explanation.

(c) Impeaching One's Own Witness

There is thought to be something wrong in a counsel calling a person as a witness and then, if the evidence is not as favourable as expected,

---

50 For provincial and territorial counterparts, see: R.S.A. 2000, c. A-18, ss. 22, 23; R.S.B.C. 1996, c. 124, ss. 13, 14; R.S.M 1987, c. E150, ss. 20 and 21; R.S.N.B. 1973, c. E-11, ss. 18 and 19; R.S.N.L. 1988, c. E-16, ss. 10-12; R.S.N.W.T. 1988, c. E-8, ss. 27, 28; R.S.N.S. 1989, c. 154, ss. 56 and 57; R.S.O. 1990, c. E.23, ss. 20 and 21; R.S.P.E.l. 1988, c. E-11, ss. 16 and 17; R.S.S. 1978, c. S-16, ss. 39 and 40; and R.S.Y. 1986, c. 57, ss. 24 and 25.

attacking the witness's credibility. There is thought to be a danger that the witness would then be at the mercy of counsel. But suppose, in preparation for trial, counsel interviews a prospective witness, that witness says he is prepared to describe the incident in a favourable way, counsel calls the witness and the witness surprises counsel and describes the matter in a completely different way. If counsel is not permitted to impeach the witness by proving the previous inconsistent statement we have counsel at the mercy of the witness. The Legislature has effected a compromise.

For criminal cases, the *Canada Evidence Act* provides:

> 9. (1) A party producing a witness shall not be allowed to impeach his credit by general evidence of bad character, but if the witness, in the opinion of the court, proves adverse, the party may contradict him by other evidence, or, by leave of the court, may prove that the witness made at other times a statement inconsistent with his present testimony, but before the last mentioned proof can be given the circumstances of the supposed statement, sufficient to designate the particular occasion, shall be mentioned to the witness, and he shall be asked whether or not he did make the statement.

> (2) Where the party producing a witness alleges that the witness made at other times a statement in writing, reduced to writing, or recorded on audio tape or video tape or otherwise, inconsistent with the witness' present testimony, the court may, without proof that the witness is adverse, grant leave to that party to cross-examine the witness as to the statement and the court may consider the cross-examination in determining whether in the opinion of the court the witness is adverse.

The legislation continues the prohibition against adducing general evidence of bad character. The legislation seems to provide that a ruling of adversity is necessary before a party can lead evidence that contradicts his previous witness but this is recognized by all as a blunder in legislative drafting and there is no such requirement.[51] There is such a requirement before a party will be permitted to prove a previous inconsistent statement of his own witness. The legislation provides that if the judge decides that the witness is adverse to the party calling him the party can impeach by proving the previous statement. Once the previous statement has been proved cross-examination can be had thereon. Adversity simply means opposed in interest. It need not amount to hostility of demeanour which as we saw earlier permits cross-examination at large.

Section 9(2) was introduced in 1969 to facilitate the finding of adversity. The cross-examination mentioned was designed to take place in the absence of the jury; it was to help the judge decide whether the witness was adverse and the party permitted to prove the earlier statement under s. 9(1). When

---

51 *Greenough v. Eccles* (1859), 141 E.R. 315 at 321.

it came to be judicially interpreted, however, it was decided that s. 9(2) was not just a preface to s. 9(1) but rather was a device unto itself providing a separate mode of impeachment; the cross-examination spoken of in s. 9(2) will take place in front of the jury if the judge determines that the previous statement was in fact inconsistent with the witness's present testimony. In *Milgaard*,[52] the Court announced the proper procedure when counsel wishes to make an application under s. 9(2): advise the court of the intention to make an application. The jury retires. Counsel produces the statement for the trial judge to read. The trial judge determines whether in fact there is an inconsistency between the statement and the evidence the witness has given. If there is no inconsistency, that's the end of the matter. If he decides there is an inconsistency counsel is called on to prove the statement. He can produce it to the witness and have the witness admit having made the statement or, if the witness does not admit it, counsel can provide the necessary proof by other evidence. Once the statement is proved, counsel for the opposing party has the right to cross-examine as to the circumstances under which the statement was made and the right to call evidence as to factors relevant to obtaining the statement for the purpose of attempting to show that cross-examination should not be permitted. The trial judge should then decide whether or not he will permit the cross-examination and, if so, the jury is recalled. The cross-examination provided for in the section will be in the presence of the jury. If the trial judge then decides and declares that the witness is adverse, s. 9(1) comes into play and the statement may be proved to the jury. The trial judge may, as the result of the cross-examination, also declare that the witness is hostile and permit cross-examination at large.[53]

In civil cases, of course, the provincial legislation applies. All provinces, except Alberta, and both Territories have legislation identical to s. 9(1) of the *Canada Evidence Act* without the s. 9(2) provision.[54] Alberta's legislation is to the same effect as the other provinces.[55] The procedure for impeachment of one's own witness in civil cases is seemingly simpler than is the case with criminal prosecutions.[56]

---

52 *R. v. Milgaard* (1971), 2 C.C.C. (2d) 206 (Sask. C.A.). The *Milgaard* view was specifically approved in *R. v. Rouse* (1978), 42 C.C.C. (2d) 481 (S.C.C.).

53 See Webster, *"Cross-examination on a Finding of Adversity"* (1995), 38 C.R. (4th) 35.

54 R.S.A. 2000, s. A-18, s. 25; R.S.B.C. 1996, c. 124, s. 16; R.S.M. 1987, c. E150, s. 19; R.S.N.B. 1973, c. E-11, s. 17; R.S.N.L. 1990, c. E-16, s. 10; R.S.N.W.T. 1988, c. E-8, s. 30; R.S.N.S. 1989, c. 154, s. 55; R.S.O. 1990, c. E.23, s. 23; R.S.P.E.I. 1988, c. E-11, s. 15; R.S.S. 1978, c. S-16, s. 38; and R.S.Y. 1986, c. 57, s. 27.

55 R.S.A. 1980, c. A-21, s. 26.

56 For instruction, see *Hanes v. Wawanesa Mutual Insurance Co.*, [1961] O.R. 495 (C.A.).

(d) Bias

Witnesses are no longer barred from testifying solely because they are interested in the outcome.[57] Feelings for or against a party, though causing the witness's testimony to be less than impartial, are not grounds for exclusion. Rather they are fruitful areas for counsel to explore for impeachment purposes. Since such feelings betray emotional partiality which may impair the witness's testimonial qualifications, evidence of the same is not collateral and counsel is entitled not only to explore those feelings on cross-examination but also to prove the same should the witness deny them. If counsel intends to impeach the witness by evidence of bias counsel is obliged to first put the question to the witness. Again it's a matter of economy and fairness. If the witness is asked about the possibility of bias and admits it, there is no need in taking up the court's time with independent proof. Also, it is fairer to ask the witness in the stand so that he might perhaps explain the appearance of bias than to surprise him afterward when he has no opportunity to respond.[58]

(e) Character of the Witness

Although it is very uncommon, it is permissible to call a witness to testify concerning another witness's character for truth-telling. The witness may testify to the other witness's bad reputation for veracity or might simply testify to his opinion that he, the impeaching witness, would not believe the other witness on his oath. This entitlement is from another age and its limited use to be appreciated.[59]

The common law has long held that independent proof of specific acts of a person impacting on that person's character for veracity was not receivable. The witness might be asked about these matters in cross-examination but it was regarded as necessary to exclude independent proof of the same to avoid undue consumption of time, confusing the issues and out of considerations of fairness to the witness. This is the collateral facts rule.[60]

The common law, however, provided that should the previous actions of the witness have resulted in a criminal conviction the same could be proved as the competing dangers were very much minimized. The previous judgment of conviction was conclusive, didn't need to be litigated and was quick to prove. Persons who had been convicted of an infamous crime were

---

57 See *R. v. Dikah* (1994), 31 C.R. (4th) 105 (Ont. C.A.).
58 See *Attorney General v. Hitchcock* (1847), 154 E.R. 38 (Exch.Ct.); and *General Films Ltd. v. McElroy,* [1939] 4 D.L.R. 543 at 549 (Sask. C.A.).
59 See *Masztalar v. Wiens* (1992), 2 C.P.C. (3d) 294 (B.C. C.A.).
60 Discussed, *supra,* Collateral Facts Limitation.

not competent as witnesses until the middle of the nineteenth century. When made competent, legislation was enacted paralleling the common law, permitting questions to the witness about previous convictions and independent proof should the witness deny the same. In Canada, our legislatures have copied this legislation. For example, the *Canada Evidence Act* provides:

> 12. (1) A witness may be questioned as to whether the witness has been convicted of any offence, excluding any offence designated as a contravention under the *Contraventions Act*, but including such an offence where the conviction was entered after a trial on an indictment.
>
> (1.1) If the witness either denies the fact or refuses to answer, the opposite party may prove the conviction.

(f) Accused as Witness

The accused was not rendered a competent witness in Canada until 1893. The accused was thought to be so interested in the outcome of the trial that he should not be heard. Also, some thought it offensive to the privilege against self-incrimination that he be placed on the horns of a dilemma and forced to choose whether or not he would take an oath in his defence; to choose short-term relief but risk eternal damnation. The enactment which made him a competent witness for the defence contained no language which would afford him any greater protection from questioning as to his previous criminal record than that available to an ordinary witness and so it was early decided by the courts.[61] The accused who chooses to become a witness, however, risks far more from this type of questioning than does the ordinary witness. The questions and independent proof should he deny the previous convictions are, in theory at least, solely referable to the accused/witness's credibility. The trier of fact, however, may use the evidence of the previous convictions as proof that the accused is the sort of person who would commit the act alleged. That use is, of course, prohibited.[62] If being tried by a jury the judge will have to instruct them that the evidence can only be used as impacting on the accused's credibility and not on his character. This limiting instruction may well be futile, particularly if the previous convictions are for activity similar to that being prosecuted.

Our courts have decided that s. 12 is subject to judicial discretion and if the trial judge decides that the probative value of the evidence of the previous convictions relative to credibility is outweighed by the possibility of unfair prejudice to the accused, evidence of the previous convictions can

---

61 *R. v. D'Aoust* (1902), 5 C.C.C. 407 at 411 (C.A.).

62 See Chapter 1, *Evidence of the Accused's Character.*

be excluded.[63] Factors that are relevant in assessing the probative value or potential prejudice of such evidence are the nature of the previous conviction and its proximity in time to the present charge. Acts of deceit, dishonesty and fraud reflect adversely on a person's credibility and honesty, while acts of violence which may result from a combative nature, and reflect on the person's propensity for violence, generally have little bearing on veracity. The more similar the offence to which the previous conviction relates to the conduct for which the accused is on trial, the greater the possibility of prejudice produced by its admission. The more distant in time the less probative value in the previous conviction. If there was a deliberate attack upon the credibility of a Crown witness it may be necessary to permit cross-examination of the accused to ensure the jury is not presented with a distorted picture but, of course, this should only be done when this would render the trial more, and not less, fair.[64]

Our courts have also decided that while witnesses generally are open to cross-examination at large as to their credit, an accused, because of his special vulnerability, aside from questions regarding previous convictions, should not be cross-examined with regard to previous misconduct or discreditable associations unrelated to the charge.[65]

(g) Primary Witness in Prosecutions of Sexual Assault

At common law, when the alleged victim testified in a rape prosecution, she could be cross-examined not only concerning the material facts but also as to her character as this was seen to reflect on her credibility. In this she was treated as any other witness. If the questions had relevance solely to her credibility, she could not be contradicted in her answers as this would offend the collateral facts rule.

The common law decided that unchasteness was relevant to credibility. Therefore she could be asked about previous sexual intercourse with the accused and with others. If asked about previous sexual intercourse with persons other than the accused, the law regarded such questions as solely referable to credibility and she could not be contradicted if she denied the same. One can imagine, however, how a jury might react simply to the

---

63 *R. v. Corbett* (1988), 64 C.R. (3d) 1 (S.C.C.). The exercise of the discretion has been uneven and many, if not most, trial judges, unfortunately, will not exclude such questioning: see *R. v. P. (G.F.)* (1994), 29 C.R. (4th) 315 (Ont. C.A.); *R. v. Bailey* (1993), 22 C.R. (4th) 65 (Ont. Gen. Div.); *R. v. Hoffman* (1994), 32 C.R. (4th) 396 (Alta. C.A.); *R. v. Saroya* (1992), 18 C.R. (4th) 198 (Ont. Gen. Div.), affirmed (1994), 76 O.A.C. 25 (C.A.); and *R. v. Brand* (1995), [1995] O.J. No. 1342, 1995 CarswellOnt 116 (C.A.).

64 For the proper procedure to follow see *R. v. Underwood* (1998), 12 C.R. (5th) 241 (S.C.C.).

65 *R. v. Davison* (1974), 20 C.C.C. (2d) 424 (Ont. C.A.). See also *R. v. Jones* (1988), 44 C.C.C. (3d) 248 (Ont. C.A.).

questions being put. If the questions were about previous sexual intercourse with the accused and the witness denied the same, evidence could be led as the common law regarded evidence of a previous sexual relationship with the accused as relevant not just to credibility but also relevant to whether the alleged victim had consented on the occasion under review and therefore independent proof of the same did not offend the collateral facts rule. The common law also decided that she could be asked about her reputation as a prostitute or for promiscuity; these questions were also regarded as not collateral and independent proof could be led with respect to them. The federal Legislature intervened in 1992 with amendments to the *Criminal Code:*

> 276. (1) In proceedings in respect of [sexual offences], evidence that the complainant has engaged in sexual activity, whether with the accused or with any other person, is not admissible to support an inference that, by reason of the sexual nature of that activity, the complainant
>
> > (a) is more likely to have consented to the sexual activity that forms the subject-matter of the charge; or
> > (b) is less worthy of belief.
>
> (2) In proceedings in respect of an offence referred to in subsection (1), no evidence shall be adduced by or on behalf of the accused that the complainant has engaged in sexual activity other than the sexual activity that forms the subject-matter of the charge, whether with the accused or with any other person, unless the judge, provincial court judge or justice determines . . .. that the evidence
>
> > (a) is of specific instances of sexual activity;
> > (b) is relevant to an issue at trial; and
> > (c) has significant probative value that is not substantially outweighed by the danger of prejudice to the proper administration of justice.
>
> . . .
>
> 277. In proceedings in respect of [sexual offences], evidence of sexual reputation, whether general or specific, is not admissible for the purpose of challenging or supporting the credibility of the complainant.[66]

The legislation also provided for a procedure for determining whether the evidence could be received under subs. (2).

On a trial of sexual assault, receiving evidence of the complainant's previous sexual history has the potential to prejudice the proper outcome of the trial. The trier may give the evidence an exaggerated probative value on the issue of consent. Alternatively, the trier might conclude, as the result of such evidence, that the complainant's worth as a person is suspect, and

---

66 R.S.C. 1985, c. C-46.

accordingly might not take their task of carefully analyzing the evidence as seriously as they should; they might not see a conviction as important as it might be seen with respect to another victim. On the other hand, a blanket exclusion of such evidence could do an injustice as it could interfere with an accused's right to make full answer and defence; the accused's rights in this regard are guaranteed by the common law, and in Canada by the *Criminal Code* and s. 7 of the *Canadian Charter of Rights and Freedoms.* To draw the appropriate line which will ensure a fair trial and at the same time protect the legitimate interests of both the complainant and the accused, the evidentiary provisions enacted by the Canadian Parliament must be read subject to an overriding discretion in the trial judge to receive evidence of the complainant's previous sexual history when the trial judge determines that the probative value of the same outweighs the possibility of prejudice to the proper outcome of the trial. So long as the inference from past to present behaviour does not rest on highly dubious beliefs about "women who do" and "women who don't", evidence of the complainant's previous sexual activity, with the accused or with another, should not be foreclosed by s. 276.[67]

(h) Defects in the Capacity of a Witness

The cross-examiner is always entitled to attempt impeachment by questioning the witness's general capacity to observe, recollect and communicate, and his particular ability in the case under review. "Witness, you say that you were able to see the accident from a distance of 50 metres. When was the last time you had your eyes checked?" Sometimes the witness will confess the possibility of error as the result of certain incapacities. If the witness denies the possibility, counsel may decide to lead extrinsic evidence to contradict. There are no hard and fast rules. The judge will decide, in her discretion, whether the probative value of the extrinsic evidence, outlined by counsel, outweighs competing considerations of time, confusion of the issues and fairness to the witness.

When a witness, because of a physical or mental defect, is not capable of giving an accurate account concerning the incident, a medical expert will be permitted to testify to this fact. If the optometrist is able to say that the witness's eyesight is so defective that he couldn't possibly have seen the incident from his position at the time he will be allowed to speak and thus

---

67 See *R. v. Osolin* (1994), 26 C.R. (4th) 1 (S.C.C.); *R. v. Ecker* (1995), 37 C.R. (4th) 51 at 72 (Sask. C.A.); and Paciocco, "The New Rape Shield Laws Should Survive Charter Challenge" (1993), 21 C.R. (4th) 223. Adopting Paciocco's interpretation of the legislation, and recognizing discretion in the trial judge, see *R. v. Darrach* (2000), 36 C.R. (5th) 223 (S.C.C.).

impeach the witness. So, too, a psychiatrist will be allowed to testify that because of the witness's mental disability his description of the matter is suspect.[68]

7. Supporting a Witness's Credibility

Speaking generally, evidence in support of a witness's credibility is not receivable, unless and until the witness's credibility has been attacked. It is not irrelevance that dictates rejection but rather superfluity. Until there has been an attack on the witness's credibility it is assumed that the witness is a credible witness and the court says it is not worth the consumption of time to lead evidence in support.

Previous consistent statements of a witness are generally inadmissible because they are seen to be superfluous. At times the courts will say that the exclusion of a previous statement consistent with the witness's present testimony is excluded because it is self-serving and there is a danger that the witness manufactured evidence for himself by making the earlier statement but the better explanation is superfluity. As with any rule of evidence, there are seen to be exceptions. The so-called exceptions might better be seen as instances when the rule does not apply because the basis of the rule doesn't exist. Nevertheless for ease of reference we will here consider them as exceptions.

(a) To Rebut the Allegation of Afterthought

If, in cross-examination, a witness's account of some incident is challenged as being a recent invention, it is not superfluous to lead evidence to rebut that suggestion by showing that at an earlier time the witness made a statement which is consistent with her present testimony. The exception operates when the trial judge in her discretion judges that there has been, or probably will be, a suggestion that the witness has recently made up the story. The allegation need not be express but may also arise implicitly from the whole circumstances of the case and the conduct of the trial.[69] At times the court might emphasize the requirement that the allegation needs to have been of a recent invention; an allegation that the witness's story has been fabricated from day one is not sufficient to trigger the exception.[70]

---

68 *Toohey v. Metropolitan Police Commissioners,* [1965] A.C. 595 at 607-608 (H.L.); and
    R. v. Dietrich (1970), 1 C.C.C. (2d) 49 (Ont. C.A.).
69 *R. v. Giraldi* (1975), 28 C.C.C. (2d) 248 (B.C. C.A.); and *R. v. Campbell* (1977), 38
    C.C.C. (2d) 6 (Ont. C.A.).
70 *R. v. Pangilinan* (1987), 60 C.R. (3d) 188 (B.C. C.A.).

(b) Prior Identification

When a witness at trial is asked to identify a person in the courtroom, the circumstances surrounding that identification may seriously weaken the weight that will be given to it by the trier of fact. When the eye-witness says that the person in the dock, sitting between two constables, is the person who did the dastardly deed, the trier might theorize that the witness is not giving his present recollection of the incident but rather that the witness is concluding from the accused's location in the courtroom that the police have arrested the proper person. Since the circumstances surrounding the witness's present in-court statement of identification cast doubt on its validity, evidence of a previous identification is not superfluous and therefore is receivable.[71]

(c) Recent Complaint

The common law decided that a complaint by a victim of sexual assault, if made at the first reasonable opportunity after the assault, was receivable in evidence. The reason, again, was that such a complaint was not regarded as superfluous. It was thought that if a woman was sexually assaulted it would be a very natural thing to complain about it. A failure to do so would be seen to contradict her allegation. If nothing was said at trial about a complaint being made then the trier might assume there was none and the credibility of the complainant would be adversely affected. Accordingly, if there was a complaint, evidence of the fact of the complaint and its details could be led to counter this assumption.[72] If there was no complaint, adverse comments by the defence counsel and by the judge could be made. More recently it has been recognized that adverse inferences from a failure to complain are unfounded as there are many reasons why a victim of sexual assault will not complain at the first opportunity. In 1983, the *Criminal Code* was amended to provide "S. 275. The rules relating to evidence of recent complaint [in sexual assault cases] are hereby abrogated."

The section is ambiguous and there have been varying interpretations of whether comment on a failure to complain is permitted.[73] It seems to be commonly understood, however, that if there was a complaint it can no longer be received under this common law exception "in the Crown's

---

71 See *R. v. Christie*, [1914] A.C. 545 at 551 (H.L.).

72 *R. v. Lillyman*, [1896] 2 Q.B. 167 (C.C.C.R.).

73 Compare *R. v. James* (1993), 24 C.R. (4th) 229 (Ont. Gen. Div.); and *R. v. Page* (1984), 40 C.R. (3d) 85 (Ont. Gen. Div.).

presentation of its case. But an accused may open the door depending on its cross-examination".[74]

(d) Narrative

There are times when the unfolding of the story for the trier of fact requires that the trier understand that statements were made which caused certain action. Receiving evidence of these statements is commonly referred to as receiving evidence of statements as part of the narrative. Until quite recently, this exception was carefully limited to those instances where it was necessary for the jury to understand the unfolding of events to be apprised of the content of statements made,[75] for example, where, in a sexual assault case, the complaint was so inextricably woven with the evidence of what happened that the case could not be otherwise properly presented.[76] It was said that at most the Crown was entitled to lead evidence that, for example, the mother contacted the police as the result of information she received from her daughter.[77] More recently, there has been a change in the law which allows that it is part of the narrative to recount the earlier complaints of the alleged victim of sexual assault as part of the narrative; this is said to be necessary to provide background to the story. The courts, perhaps aware of the major change they have effected, insist that the trier must then be admonished not to use the earlier statements as confirming the present allegation but only to assist them in understanding what happened.[78]

One court has recognized that where the witness is a child, it may not be redundant to lead evidence of an earlier out-of-court consistent statement as the best way to gain a full account of what happened and to rebut commonly held beliefs about children being less than credible.[79] If the basis of exclusion of previous statements is superfluity, with children it may not be superfluous to hear what they earlier reported and such statements deserve receipt.

---

74 *R. v. O'Connor* (1995), 100 C.C.C. (3d) 285 (Ont. C.A.).
75 *R. v. Albert* (1993), 19 C.R. (4th) 322 (Ont. C.A.).
76 *R. v. Cassibo* (1982), 70 C.C.C. (2d) 498 (Ont. C.A.).
77 *R. v. Jones, supra,* note 65.
78 *R. v. F. (J.E.)* (1993), 26 C.R. (4th) 220 (Ont. C.A.); *R. v. Ay* (1994), 93 C.C.C. (3d) 456 (B.C. C.A.); *R. v. B. (O.)* (1995), [1995] N.S.J. No. 499, 1995 CarswellNS 244 (C.A.); and *R. v. Foster* (1995), 128 Sask. R. 292 (C.A.), leave to appeal refused (1996), 152 Sask. R. 316 (note) (S.C.C.).
79 *R. v. B. (D.C.)* (1994), 32 C.R. (4th) 91 (Man. C.A.).

(e) Expert Evidence

Our courts decided that, while an expert could testify to impeach credibility, it was wrong to permit an expert to testify in support. It was frequently said that to do so was to revert to the middle ages concept of oath-helping.[80] Recently, however, our courts have recognized that experts can, in certain cases, be helpful. Experts are now permitted to testify about certain observed phenomena that are commonly found to exist with respect to certain individuals. Expert opinion about the general behavioural and psychological characteristics of child victims of sexual abuse is admissible to assist a trier of fact in coming to a conclusion as to credibility. Expert evidence about the general behaviour patterns of children in circumstances similar to the alleged victim could be helpful. For example, in a prosecution for sexual assault on a child, where her credibility was attacked because she had, before trial, written a letter denying the truth of her allegations, it was permissible to hear from an expert that it was not uncommon for victims of sexual abuse to recant their allegations. That would be a fact not generally known to the lay person.[81] Should a victim of sexual assault be attacked in her credibility because she frequently recounted fantastic stories of abuse, she might be rehabilitated by expert advice that such accounts are a symptom of sexual abuse.[82] Should an alleged victim be attacked in her credibility because she told a different story exonerating the accused on an earlier occasion, she might be rehabilitated by expert evidence that child victims frequently fabricate such excusing stories and for the expert to explain why that is so.[83] Where a victim's credibility was doubted because he did not report the abuse for a period of time and continued to associate with the offender, an expert was permitted to rehabilitate with testimony that these facts were not necessarily inconsistent with the truth of the allegations and to explain why.[84] However our highest Court has recently challenged the admissibility of expert evidence on delayed disclosure saying that such evidence is unnecessary and ought to be dealt with by a simple jury instruction from the trial judge.[85] All of this expert evidence is receivable as long as the expert does not cross over the line and give her opinion that the particular witness before the court is telling the truth.

---

80   *R. v. Kyselka* (1962), 133 C.C.C. 103 (Ont. C.A.); and *R. c. Béland* (1987), 60 C.R. (3d) 1 (S.C.C.).

81   *R. v. J. (F.E.), supra,* note 18.

82   *R. v. T. (S.)* (1986), 31 C.C.C. (3d) 1 (Ont. C.A.).

83   *R. v. Marquard, supra,* note 14.

84   *R. v. C. (R.A.)* (1990), 57 C.C.C. (3d) 522 (B.C. C.A.).

85   See *R. v. D. (D.)* (2000), 36 C.R. (5th) 261 (S.C.C.).

8. Corroboration

The ecclesiastical and civil law systems of proof provided that a verdict could not be had on the strength of one witness's testimony. For most issues, two witnesses were required. In addition, particular witnesses, because of their station in life, would be assigned a fractional value. The common law generally resisted this quantitative method and a single witness of quality was sufficient. There were exceptions.

(a) Perjury

In a prosecution for perjury in the common law courts, one witness was not sufficient unless there was other evidence which corroborated the witness in a material particular that implicated the accused. This requirement may be seen to be a historical accident. Perjury had been prosecuted in the Court of Star Chamber which had followed ecclesiastical procedures. When that Court was abolished in 1641, and perjury was taken over by the common law courts, the long-established procedure was incorporated. That practice, requiring corroboration in a perjury prosecution, found its way into our *Criminal Code:*

> 133. No person shall be convicted of an offence [of perjury] on the evidence of only one witness unless the evidence of that witness is corroborated in a material particular by evidence that implicates the accused.

(b) Treason

A statute enacted in England in 1547 required two witnesses for a treason prosecution. It was said that this was necessary protection against allegations of fictitious conspiracies. The *Criminal Code* continues the requirement:

> 47. (3) No person shall be convicted of high treason or treason on the evidence of only one witness, unless the evidence of that witness is corroborated in a material particular by evidence that implicates the accused.

(c) Accomplices

A wise trial judge once commented on the evidence of an accomplice in his case. He told the jury that this witness, being an accomplice of the accused, might be purchasing immunity from prosecution by giving evidence for the prosecution against his former partner. This motive should be taken into account in assessing the worth of the witness's testimony. The wise judge probably advised the jury that it was unsafe to convict on the evidence of this accomplice unless the evidence was *corroborated.* This might be sensible advice in a particular case but the law requiring such an instruction in each case involving accomplice testimony, and the magic formula of words demanded, became unduly and unnecessarily complex. The trial judge was obliged to warn the jury that there needed to be independent testimony which implicated the accused and confirmed the witness's story in some material way. The trial judge was obliged to review with the jury the evidence in the case that could amount to corroboration. Thankfully our courts have called a halt to that practice. It is not a mandatory warning in all cases but rather a matter for the trial judge to decide what sort of warning might be appropriate in his particular cases.[86] Our courts, recognizing the need for caution with respect to accepting the evidence of an accomplice, have also decided that such a caution, such a warning, might be appropriate where the witness, although not an accomplice, is disreputable or unsavoury.[87]

(d) Primary Witnesses in Sexual Assault Cases

For generations our courts expressed concern over the worth of a complainant's testimony in prosecutions for sexual assault. It was said that such an accusation was easily made and hard to defend,[88] and that sexual cases were particularly subject to the danger of false charges.[89] The common law began to insist on the same type of warning about the evidence of complainants in sexual assault cases as it had respecting the evidence of accomplices. These attitudes found their way into our *Criminal Code.* Section 142 formerly required that the trial judge, in cases of rape, attempted rape, sexual intercourse with a female under 16 and indecent assault, proceed in the following manner:

> If the only evidence that implicates the accused is the evidence, given under oath, of the female person in respect of whom the offence is alleged to have been committed and that evidence is not corroborated in a material particular by evidence that implicates the accused, instruct the jury that it is not safe to find the accused guilty in the absence of such corroboration.

Section 139 provided that with respect to certain sexual offences a conviction could not be had unless there was corroboration. In these instances a warning was not sufficient; a conviction was barred. These provisions have now been repealed but it is debatable whether the attitudes

---

86 *R. v. Vetrovec* (1982), 67 C.C.C. (2d) 1 (S.C.C.).
87 *R. v. Brooks* (2000), 30 C.R. (5th) 201 (S.C.C.).
88 *Hale, Pleas of the Crown* (1680) at 633.
89 G. Williams, "Corroboration", [1962] Crim. L. Rev. 662.

toward the evidence of complainants have changed. Legislation can only do so much.[90]

(e) Unsworn Evidence of Children

The *Canada Evidence Act* and the *Criminal Code* had, until quite recently, provisions mandating corroboration if the evidence of the child was given unsworn. Indeed, even if the evidence was given sworn, the law appeared to require that a warning be given to the jury about the frailties of children's evidence.[91] As we saw earlier, when dealing with the recent changes in the federal legislation concerning the oath, warnings concerning the evidence of children is still mandated. Some provincial *Evidence Acts* have been changed to mirror the federal scene[92] but others,[93] still requiring corroboration, remain.

---

90 See e.g. *R. v. S. (F.)* (1997), 116 C.C.C. (3d) 435 (Ont. C.A.).
91 *R. v. Horsburgh,* [1968] 2 C.C.C. 288 (S.C.C.) and *R. v. S. (W.)* (1994), 29 C.R. (4th) 143 (Ont. C.A.), leave to appeal refused (1994), 35 C.R. (4th) 402 (note) (S.C.C.).
92 See *supra,* note 13.
93 See *supra,* note 10.

4

Hearsay

1. Introduction

The hearsay rule came into existence at the end of the seventeenth century. By then the adversary system had become established. The parties had taken control over who would be called as witnesses. It made sense that a witness called by one party should be open for testing for worth by questions from the opposing party. Thus came into being the notion of cross-examination which is peculiar to the common law tradition. With that development the hearsay rule could not be far behind. The law of hearsay is predicated on the thought that the adversary should have the right to test by cross-examination the validity of any description of the material event. If the person with knowledge of that event is not present in the witness stand, the adversary is frustrated. The conduct of a fair trial in the adversary system requires that the person with knowledge relate the story in open court.

The description of a past event by any witness has resident within it the possibility of error due to four dangers. First, the witness's description may be defective because the witness did not perceive the event accurately. Second, the witness when describing the event may not have then correctly remembered his earlier observation of the event. Third, the witness in describing the event may have been ambiguous or misleading in the language he chose. Fourth, the witness may have been insincere and deliberately wished to mislead. To have the witness's story related by another is regarded as unfair. That other cannot describe why the description of the event is accurate as he is unable to answer any questions from the adversary concerning its accuracy. The adversary cannot test whether the person who actually witnessed the event had able powers of perception, whether that person's description of the event was rendered at a time when the event was fresh in that person's memory, whether the words used to describe the incident are properly understood in the sense that the person intended and whether the person who observed the event was motivated to give a true rendition. Those possibilities, those dangers, cannot be explored unless the witness himself is in the witness stand. These are the "hearsay dangers": perception, memory, sincerity and communication.[1]

Another, distinct, reason for insisting on the presence in the courtroom of the person with actual knowledge has to do with the jury's capacity to adequately assess the worth of the description. The jury, the trier of fact, will be more assured of accuracy in their decision if the description of the event is given in open court by the person with knowledge and not through an intermediary. The presence in the courtroom of the person with the knowledge will enhance trustworthiness. The witness who speaks in open court knows that he is subject to a perjury prosecution should he lie. The witness who speaks in open court is encouraged to speak honestly without exaggeration by the solemnity of the occasion and by the presence of the party against whose interests he speaks. The witness, if in open court, will be open to examination as to his demeanour, his manner of speaking, and the trier of fact will therefore be better able to evaluate his credibility.

And so we say that it is not right for a witness to relate what he or she has *heard* another *say*. The *hearsay* rule refers to statements that a witness has heard another make about the matter. That is prohibited. It does not signify, though an intelligent argument could otherwise be maintained, that the person who observed the event must be *here* to *say* what happened. The rule is the *hearsay* rule and not the *heresay* rule.

2. Identifying Hearsay

Not all out-of-court statements are deserving of the label hearsay. The principal reasons for excluding hearsay evidence are the lack of the protective safeguards of oath and cross-examination, safeguards which are only necessary when the value of the evidence depends on the credibility of the asserter.[2] If the value of the out-of-court statement rests not on the credibility of the asserter, but has value resident solely in the fact that the statement was made, there can be no hearsay objection to the introduction of such a statement.

A sues B for failure to deliver lumber in accordance with their contract. B defends, denying the existence of any contract. A calls X to testify that he heard B unequivocally and unambiguously agreeing to deliver lumber to A on a certain date for a certain price. Clearly this is not hearsay. We care not whether B was sincere in expressing his intention to accept the terms. The legal consequences of a valid contract are produced by the fact

1 Morgan, "Hearsay Dangers and the Application of the Hearsay Concept" (1948) Harv. Law Rev. 177.
2 See McCormick, *Evidence*, 2d Edition (1972), p. 584.

that B spoke the words. The value of the words does not rest on the credibility of the out-of-court asserter. B's out-of-court statement is not hearsay.

Similarly, proof of statements constituting defamation would not offend the hearsay rule. The plaintiff who complains that he was defamed by the defendant's out-of-court statement and seeks to prove that the defendant made the statement is obviously not attempting to prove the truth asserted within the statements. The value of the statement resides solely in the fact that the statement was made.

Words accompanying actions often characterize the same and, if the substantive law has an objective test of intention, the words are receivable. "I give this land to you for your use and for the use of your heirs." If the substantive law of property characterizes such a transaction as a gift when the donor's intention is manifested by words the value of the statement rests solely in the fact that the statement was made. Statements made by suspects in a criminal case during the course of a police investigation, which statements are established to be false, may be received as non-hearsay evidencing a consciousness of guilt on the part of the speakers. The accused who seeks to rely on the defence of provocation is able to relate for the court what another said to him that caused him to react in the manner in which he did. The list of situations of relevant non-hearsay statements, and their variety, is limitless, and their identification is only eased when the purpose of the hearsay rule is kept in the forefront. The hearsay rule is designed to protect the adversary against the admission of evidence which cannot be tested by the adversary as to its worth.

Identifying whether an out-of-court statement is hearsay or not is seen by many as a difficult exercise and various formulae of words have been used for the purpose. One popular formula, which however is problematic, is to ask whether the statement is being tendered for its truth or tendered for the fact that the statement was made. Although this is perhaps a fair description, the formula frequently produces circumlocutions that confound. It is not unusual for counsel to seek an end run around the hearsay rule by insisting that he is not tendering the evidence for the purpose of establishing its truth but rather only for the purpose of establishing that the statement was in fact made. When counsel offers this in justification, the adversary should ask the proponent of the evidence to precisely articulate the relevance in the case resident in the fact that the statement was made. It will often be seen that the only relevance that can be found will reside in accepting the speaker's belief concerning an external event as accurate; the statement will be seen to be of value only if we assume its truth. The statement on close analysis will often be seen to be hearsay.

An example might assist. Dante is charged with the robbery of Harold. When Dante was arrested, he was taken to a detention centre and booked in. Investigating Officer King has testified that the victim Harold gave him a list of the serial numbers of the bills taken from him in the robbery. Harold had made the list just before the robbery. King went to the detention centre and, on examining the booking sheet, observed that when Dante was booked in certain personal effects were taken from him. He asked to see those effects. He was given an envelope which had the name "Dante" written thereon. In the envelope were found two bills with serial numbers matching numbers on the list provided by Harold. Harold is prepared to testify, refreshing his memory from the list that he prepared, that these two bills were part of the money taken from him during the robbery. Dante attacks the evidence as hearsay. The Crown argues that the evidence is not hearsay. The Crown argues that the name "Dante" on the envelope is not an out-of-court statement being tendered for the purpose of proving its truth. It is evidence only that the statement was in fact made. The fact that the statement was made is a piece of original circumstantial evidence from which the trier of fact can infer that the two bills were in Dante's possession when he was arrested. This is quite an attractive argument, at least on the surface, and might be accepted.[3] But analyze the situation. How is the fact that the name "Dante" appears on the envelope relevant to the issue? Someone, probably the booking officer, wrote the name "Dante" on the envelope. The fact of the name appearing, the fact that the statement was made, only has relevance if we accept that the writer was accurate when he identified these effects as belonging to Dante. If the booking officer had written on the envelope "I found the contents of this envelope on the person of Dante when he arrived at the booking office" all would quickly see that this was a hearsay statement. The worth of the statement depended on the credibility of the out-of-court asserter, the booking officer, and the adversary, Dante, was prevented from challenging, through cross-examination, the worth of the out-of-court statement.[4]

A better analytical technique for determining whether a statement is hearsay would be framed in terms of the underlying concern of the rule. As with the proper application of all rules of evidence, it is wise to always keep in mind the purpose of the rule. Given the basis for the hearsay rule — the adversary's inability to cross-examine the person with knowledge of the event — we can then construct an analytical tool for identifying hearsay. If there are relevant, meaningful questions that the adversary might wish to ask of the person who made the out-of-court statement, then the out-of-court statement is hearsay; if there are no meaningful questions that can be

---

3   For judicial acceptance of such an argument, see *R. v. Bastien* (1968), 20 C.C.C. (2d) 562 (B.C. Co. Ct.).

4   For judicial recognition that this is the proper analysis, see *R. v. Lal* (1979), 51 C.C.C. (2d) 336 (B.C. C.A.).

put, the statement is not hearsay. To properly identify whether or not an out-of-court statement is hearsay keep in mind the reason for the rule.

A classic example of the problem of identification, taken from the cases, might assist in a better understanding of this technique. In *Subramaniam*,[5] the accused had been convicted of unlawfully possessing ammunition thereby assisting the terrorist enemy. He was sentenced to death. His defence had been duress and he had sought to relate conversations he had had with the terrorists who had threatened him. The terrorists had, according to the accused, told him that he would be shot if he didn't help them. The Trial Court ruled this evidence was hearsay, and not admissible unless the terrorists were called. On appeal this was held to be error. The appellate Court noted that evidence of a statement made to a witness by a person who is not himself called as a witness is hearsay and inadmissible only when the object of the evidence was to establish the truth of what was contained in the statement. The Court recognized that in this case the fact that the statement was made, quite apart from its truth, was relevant in considering the mental state and conduct of the accused to whom the statement was made. The trier of fact would not be misled, nor the adversary prejudiced, by the absence from the witness stand of the terrorist-declarant. Using the suggested method of identifying whether or not an out-of-court statement is hearsay, ask yourself whether there are any meaningful questions that the adversary, the prosecution, might want to put to the out-of-court terrorist-declarant. If the terrorist were called as a witness, what questions would the adversary ask? Could the adversary ask the terrorist if he was sincere when he threatened the accused? If he intended to communicate a threat? Surely those questions would be properly objected to as immaterial since the issue before the Court was not the terrorist's state of mind but rather the accused's. Since it was the fact of the statement having been made that was relevant, since there were no meaningful questions that the adversary could put, the adversary would be protected and trustworthiness assured by allowing the accused to testify; the accused is on oath and may be cross-examined regarding his sincerity, perception and memory concerning whether the statement was in fact made and whether he was in fear as a result.[6]

3. Implied Assertions

Out-of-court statements can be made otherwise than by words. A nod of the head can communicate assent as readily as the spoken word "yes";

---

5 *Subramaniam v. Public Prosecutor*, [1956] 1 W.L.R. 965 (Malaya P.C.).

6 Even experts in the law of evidence can be fooled; see the contrasting opinions of Judges Sopinka and McLachlin in *R. v. Dipietro* (1993), (sub nom. *R. v. Evans*) 25 C.R. (4th) 46 (S.C.C.).

pointing to a suspect can be as communicative as the statement "that is the man". Actions which are intended by the actor to be assertions are therefore as capable of attracting hearsay analysis as verbal utterances.

But what of implied assertions? What of conduct which was not intended by the actor to be assertive of anything but from which an onlooker might draw an inference regarding the actor's beliefs? Should we subject such conduct to hearsay requirements? An example might assist. A ship was lost at sea. All hands were lost. In a civil suit brought against an insurance company the claim is resisted on the basis that the ship was not seaworthy when it sailed. The plaintiff wants to introduce into evidence the fact that before the ship sailed the captain examined the vessel. He then sailed off in it with his family. The plaintiff says this is circumstantial evidence from which the trier can infer that the ship was seaworthy. The defendant insurance company maintains that the conduct of the sea captain amounts to an implied assertion by the captain that he regarded the vessel as seaworthy and his conduct only has meaning in the case if we accept the captain's belief as accurate. The defendant argues that if the captain had said, prior to his departure, "I regard this ship as seaworthy", all would agree such a statement would be labelled hearsay and the fact the assertion is implied rather than express should make no difference. The defendant says he will be prejudiced if the evidence is received because he will be unable to cross-examine the captain. How should a judge rule?

The problem has confounded law students, lawyers and judges for generations. It is perhaps a blessing that the problem is so seldom recognized. But now and then it rears its ugly head. The most recent example of its recognition in England provides classic, logical reasoning, but, some might say, an absurd result. In *Kearley*,[7] the police had raided the accused's flat. They found drugs but not in sufficient quantities to justify an inference that the accused was a dealer. The accused was taken down to the station. Over the next few hours, in the accused's absence, the police took telephone calls asking for the accused and asking to buy drugs; there were also seven callers at the door similarly interested. At his trial on charges of possession with intent to supply, the Crown called the police officers to testify to the phone calls and the visitors received. The defence unsuccessfully objected that this evidence was hearsay. The accused was convicted and his appeal dismissed. The House of Lords, however, allowed the accused's appeal. The Lords were divided. The majority ruled the evidence was hearsay and inadmissible. The minority cried out that "laymen would say the law is an ass"[8] but the majority replied that "a common sense approach is not nec-

---

7 *R. v. Kearley*, [1992] 2 All E. R. 345.
8 *Ibid., per* Lord Griffiths at 348.

essarily a reliable guide in a criminal trial,"[9] to which the reader might say "especially when dealing with the law of hearsay!"[10]

4. Exceptions to the Hearsay Rule

After the hearsay rule came into existence, judges began to create, for a variety of reasons, exceptions thereto. Depending on who is counting, the number of exceptions ranges from 22 to 28. Each has their own individual parameters and we'll examine many of the more important ones. Professor Wigmore, looking back at all these exceptions, sought a theory to explain them and to bring some coherence to the list. Generally speaking, he came up with the thought that usually there were grounds of necessity and circumstantial guarantees underlying the exceptions. Very recently, in addition to the list of exceptions which we will shortly canvass, our courts have begun to recognize a discretionary approach to the rule, based on principle.

(a) A Principled Discretionary Approach to Hearsay

The Supreme Court of Canada decided that to receive a hearsay statement into evidence it is not essential that it fit within an established exception. Relying on the principles described by Professor Wigmore, the Court cast off the shackles of the past in the groundbreaking decision of *Khan*.[11] That decision was later characterized by the Court as "the triumph of a principled analysis over a set of ossified judicially created categories."[12] *Khan* was a sexual assault case, in which the infant complainant described the criminal act to her mother shortly after it occurred. The child was not permitted to testify at trial, and the issue was whether her mother would be permitted to testify as to the statements made to her. The Court decided the statement did not fit within a recognized exception but announced that it could be received if the trial judge found grounds of necessity and circumstantial guarantees of trustworthiness. If the proponent of the evidence could persuade the trial judge that there were circumstances surrounding the making of the out-of-court statement giving sufficient guarantees of trustworthiness that cross-examination was not necessary and that there was no other way of gaining the evidence, the statement might then deserve receipt even

---

9   *Ibid., per* Lord Oliver at 370.
10 In *R. v. Edwards* (1994), 34 C.R. (4th) 113 (Ont. C.A.), affirmed (1996), 45 C.R. (4th) 307 (S.C.C.) the court took the view that incoming calls asking to purchase narcotics were not hearsay.
11 *R. v. Khan* (1990), 79 C.R. (3d) 1 (S.C.C.).
12 *R. v. Smith, infra,* note 18.

if the proponent could not fit it within one of the particular exceptions created by the courts in the eighteenth and nineteenth centuries.

The first question will be whether reception of the hearsay statement is necessary. Necessity of this nature might arise in a number of situations: the declarant whose out-of-court statement is offered may be dead, out of the jurisdiction, insane, or otherwise unavailable. But necessity, according to our courts, is not to here be equated only with the unavailability of the declarant. Necessity for these purposes is interpreted by the courts as "reasonably necessary".[13] For example, in the case of an out-of-court statement by a child, the inadmissibility of the child's evidence might be one basis for a finding of necessity; if the child is regarded as not competent to testify, her earlier statement may be seen as necessary. But even if she could testify, evidence based on psychological assessments that testimony in court might be traumatic for the child or harm the child might also serve to establish necessity.[14] Indeed, even though the child has testified, the trial judge might determine that it is reasonably necessary to admit the out-of-court statement in order to obtain an accurate and frank rendition of the child's version of the relevant events.[15] The criterion of necessity is to be given a flexible definition, capable of encompassing diverse situations. The courts have also said that necessity might be found if the out-of-court statement is such that one could not expect to get evidence of the same value in any other way; it is recognized that this type of "necessity" might actually be better characterized as expediency or convenience.[16]

The second question concerns reliability. The court needs to be satisfied that the traditional dangers associated with hearsay evidence — perception, memory, communication and sincerity — are minimal because of the circumstances surrounding the making of the statement and that the absence of cross-examination would affect only the weight to be given to the evidence and not admissibility. This decision, a judgment call entirely dependent on the circumstances of each case, illustrates the potential difficulty with the principled discretionary approach. There is a serious risk that trial judges will differ greatly in applying the elastic standard of equivalent trustworthiness and the lack of uniformity will make preparation for trial difficult.[17]

Consider for example the decision in *Smith*.[18] The accused was charged with murder. It was the theory of the Crown that Smith had accompanied

---

13   *R. v. Khan, supra*, note 11.
14   *Ibid.*
15   *Khan v. College of Physicians & Surgeons (Ontario)* (1992), 9 O.R. (3d) 641 (C.A.).
16   *R. v. B. (K. G.)* (1993), 19 C.R. (4th) 1 (S.C.C.).
17   For contrasting inclusive and exclusive approaches see *R. v. Kharsekin* (1994), 30 C.R. (4th) 252 (Nfld. C.A.) and *R. v. Cassidy* (1993), 26 C.R. (4th) 252 (Ont. Gen. Div.).
18   *R. v. Smith*, [1992] 2 S.C.R. 915.

the victim, K., from Detroit across the Canada-U.S. border to London. The Crown's theory was that Smith had tried to persuade K. to help him smuggle narcotics across the border. K. had refused. Smith had abandoned K. but had later returned, left London with K. and later murdered her. Her body was found near a service station. K. had made three phone calls to her mother that evening. The first two phone calls were made from K.'s hotel room in London. In the first call, at 10:20 p.m., K. told her mother that Smith had abandoned her and she needed a ride home. In the second call, at 11:20 p.m., K. said she was still in need of a ride. The third call was made from a pay telephone in the hotel lobby. In this call, K. told her mother that Smith had returned and therefore she did not need a ride home. Our highest Court decided that the first two calls were receivable in evidence but not the third. The Court decided that the trier of fact could properly evaluate the evidence of the first two phone calls and that the lack of cross-examination would only affect weight and not admissibility. The Court decided, however, that there were not sufficient circumstantial guarantees of trustworthiness that would justify admission of the third phone call without the possibility of cross-examination. The Court decided that K. might have been mistaken in identifying Smith as having returned or that K. deliberately wanted to mislead her mother. One can imagine another judge, in his or her discretion, deciding that the jury could similarly decide what weight should be given to the third phone call as to the first two.[19] The dangers which caused this Court to reject might be reasonably seen by another to affect weight rather than admissibility.

For better or for ill our courts have decided that in assessing the threshold reliability of the statement the judge should not look beyond the circumstances surrounding the making of the statement.[20] Although other evidence in the case might confirm the accuracy of the statement our courts have decided it would be wrong to bootstrap on the trustworthiness of other evidence at the trial in determining admissibility. If the statement is ruled admissible under the principled approach, without considering the other evidence, if the judge decides it satisfies the threshold of reliability to permit the trier of fact to consider the statement, the trier will be able to consider all of the evidence in determining the ultimate reliability of the statement.

In *B. (K.G.)*,[21] the principal Crown witnesses recanted their earlier statements to the police identifying the accused as the murderer. The Supreme Court decided that it could apply the *Khan/Smith* approach and that

---

19 On the retrial, the accused, Smith, was acquitted. The jury during their deliberations asked the judge why it was they could hear the contents of the first two calls but not the third!

20 See *R. v. Conway* (1998), 13 C.R. (5th) 139 (Ont. C.A.) and *R. v. Starr* (2000), 36 C.R. (5th) 1 (S.C.C.).

21 *R. v. B. (K.G.)*, *supra*, note 16.

the earlier statements could be given truth bearing quality. The Court placed great weight on the fact that at the trial the declarants were present as witnesses and were subject to cross-examination on their earlier statements. The Court later recognized[22] that where a witness does not recall making the earlier statement, or refuses to answer questions, the trial judge should take into account that the inability in the adversary to cross-examine might impede the jury's ability to assess the ultimate reliability of the statement.[23]

In exercising discretion in this area, there is authority for the proposition that, given the accused's right to make full answer and defence, guaranteed by s. 7 of the Charter, the court should be more willing to receive hearsay statements under *Khan/Smith* where the same will exculpate.[24]

Our highest Court has also decided that the existing exceptions must also be in accord with the principled, discretionary approach.[25] This raises an interesting question concerning which there are competing schools of thought; should a judge apply the principled approach or the exception approach first?[26]

(b) Admissions

(i) *Generally*

Perhaps the most frequently used exception to the hearsay rule is the admission. It helps that it's also the easiest to identify. An admission is, very simply, a statement made by a party when tendered by the opposing party. The purpose of the hearsay rule is to protect the adversary against the admission of evidence that the adversary cannot cross-examine. An adversary can hardly complain about the introduction of his own statements. He surely cannot object that he had no opportunity to cross-examine himself! It just seems fair, given our adversarial system, that one adversary is able

---

22 *R. v. U. (F.J.)*, [1995] 3 S.C.R. 764.

23 But see *R. v. Campbell* (2002), 1 C.R. (6th) 343 (N.S. C.A.) that " the absence of an opportunity to cross-examine the declarant does not preclude admission of the statement." See also Delisle, *B. (K.G.) and Its Progeny*, (1998) 14 C.R. (5th) 75 and Delisle, *Diu: Inconsistency in B. (K.G.) Rulings* (2000) 33 C.R. (5th) 259.

24 *R. v. Finta* (1992), 14 C.R. (4th) 1 (Ont. C.A.), affirmed [1994] 1 S.C.R. 701, application for re-hearing refused (June 23, 1994), Doc. 23023, 23097 (S.C.C.).

25 See *R. v. Starr* (2000), 36 C.R. (5th) 1 (S.C.C.).

26 Compare *R. v. Kimberly* (2001), 45 C.R. (5th) 273 (Ont. C.A.), leave to appeal refused (2002), 2002 CarswellOnt 1895, 2002 CarswellOnt 1896, [2002] S.C.C.A. No. 29 (S.C.C.) and *R. v. West* (2001), 45 C.R. (5th) 307 (Ont. S.C.J.) to *R. v. Wilcox* (2001), [2001] N.S.J. No. 85, 2001 CarswellNS 83 (C.A.). See also, Delisle, *Annotation to Kimberley*, (2001) 45 C.R.(5th) 276. See generally Stuesser, *Starr and Reform of the Hearsay Exceptions*, (2001) Can.Crim.L.R. 55 and Stewart, *Hearsay After Starr*, (2001) Can. Crim. L.R. 55.

to use any statement made by his opposite number which is relevant to a material issue.

The out-of-court statement need not have been seen by the maker to be against his interest when he made it and we don't have to worry as to whether it's against his interest when introduced at trial as we can rest assured that his opponent thinks so. There is therefore no need to style this exception as an admission against interest; an admission will do. Also, there is no absolute requirement that the maker of the statement be himself possessed of personal knowledge of the facts he has cared to admit. Since the reason for this particular exception is fairness and the adversary system, as opposed to circumstantial guarantees of trustworthiness, it is seen to be fair to receive the statement as long as the maker earlier adopted it or indicated his belief in its truth.[27] For example, in *Stowe*,[28] the plaintiff sought damages from the railway for the loss of his horse which had been hit by the defendant's train. The plaintiff was not present at the time of the accident but he had been heard to say that his brother had left open the gate to the corral. Though the plaintiff had no personal knowledge of this fact, his statement was received against him.

Continuing the thought of fairness, if one adversary chooses to use the other's statement he must use all of it. He cannot pick and choose. It would be manifestly unfair, for example, if the prosecutor introduced the accused's statement "I killed him . . ." and failed to also introduce the closing words ". . . but I didn't mean to."[29] Once the statement has been introduced it is evidence in the case and both sides are entitled to make of it what they will.

By definition, an admission is only receivable in evidence against the person who made it. If, therefore, two persons are sued for negligence in the operation of a motor vehicle, and one gave a statement admitting fault, and that statement implicated his co-defendant, the statement though receivable is not evidence against the silent co-defendant.[30] The judge needs to give a limiting instruction to the jury to that effect. The better practice is to give the instruction immediately after the statement is introduced.

When a statement is tendered as an admission against an accused in a criminal case there is another rule that must be faced. An admission by an accused is a confession and there are additional conditions of admissibility. These are canvassed in the final Chapter of this book.

---

27   *R. v. Streu*, [1989] 1 S.C.R. 1521; and *R. v. Schmidt*, [1948] S.C.R. 333.

28   *Stowe v. Grand Trunk Pacific Railway*, [1918] 1 W.W.R. 546 (Alto. C.A.), affirmed (1918), 59 S.C.R. 665.

29   See *Capital Trust Corp. v. Fowler* (1921), 64 D.L.R. 289 at 292 (Ont. C.A.). See also *R. v. Ferris* (1994), 27 C.R. (4th) 141 (Alto. C.A.), affirmed [1994] 3 S.C.R. 756; and *R. v. Phillips* (1995), [1995] O.J. No. 1360, 1996 CarswellOnt 1424.

30   *R. v. Schmidt*, [1945] S.C.R. 438; and *Chote v. Rowan*, [1943] O.W.N. 646 (C.A.).

(ii) Statements Adopted by a Party's Conduct

If an accusation is made against a party, in circumstances where it would be reasonable to expect a denial should that party regard the accusation as untrue, the party's failure to deny or protest will be received into evidence as an implied admission.[31] It needs to be emphasized that this exception does not cover all statements made in the accused's presence, although that is frequently how the exception is characterized in the courtroom. The circumstances need to be such that a protest is the reasonable thing to expect. Thus it would not be reasonable to take an accused's silence in the face of an accusation by a police officer as an acceptance as to its truth.[32] A good rule of practice is to not allow the evidence of the accusation until the proper foundation has been laid; the judge should ensure that there is evidence from which a jury could reasonably infer that the accused by his conduct in the circumstances accepted the statement as to make it his own.[33]

(iii) Statements Authorized by a Party

A person may expressly authorize another to conduct his affairs for him. When he authorizes him to act he authorizes him to speak on his behalf. Any statement made by his agent on the principal's behalf will then be receivable against the principal as a vicarious admission should litigation later follow.

If a person in the employ of another was not explicitly authorized to speak on behalf of the principal, the law of evidence has decided that an out-of-court statement made by the employee will nevertheless be receivable against the principal provided the statement was made in the course of the employment and provided it would be reasonable for the court to imply authority to speak. Just as the law of agency, or of master-servant, has constructed vicarious liability for tort based on an assessment of the agent's duties, so too the law of evidence will find a vicarious admission applying the same tests.[34] Just as vicarious liability in tort will be found if the agent or servant was acting within the scope of his duties or employment, so too authority will be found to speak on the principal's behalf. While it may not be seen as appropriate to fix a corporation with responsibility for the statement of an office boy concerning a bond issue, it might be appropriate to fix an employer with responsibility for a statement by his truck driver

---

31   *R. v. Christie*, [1914] A.C. 545 (H.L.); and *R. v. Conlon* (1990), 1 O.R. (3d) 188 (C.A.).
32   *R. v. Eden*, [1970] 2 O.R. 161 (C.A.).
33   *R. v. Harrison*, [1946] 3 D.L.R. 690 at 696 (B.C. C.A.).
34   *R. v. Strand Electric Ltd.*, [1969] 1 O.R. 190 (C.A.), *per* Laskin J.

concerning his careless driving.[35] At one time[36] it was thought that to be admissible the agent's admission needed to have been made to a third party but the better view, that it is receivable as an admission even if it was made by the agent to his own principal, has now been accepted.[37]

In a partnership each partner, when acting within the scope of the partnership, is an agent for the other partners and for the partnership. Statements made by a partner while conducting the firm's business are therefore receivable as admissions against the partnership.

It is important to recognize that before there can be vicarious responsibility for any of the above statements, the fact of the agency relationship, the preliminary condition of admissibility, must be independently established. It would, of course, be a bootstrap operation of the first order, and not acceptable if the out-of-court statements were themselves tendered as evidence of the agency relationship.[38]

(iv) Statements of Persons with a Common Purpose

When a partnership is formed for the purpose of carrying out a criminal enterprise, we commonly refer to the same as a conspiracy. The acts and statements of co-conspirators are receivable against their partners in crime if the same were done or said in furtherance of the conspiracy. The latter condition is very important. Statements by co-conspirators afterwards, in the form of narrative describing their mutual exercise, are not receivable under this head. Such statements are only receivable against their maker. The reception of co-conspirator's statements against the others is justified on the basis that each partner to the conspiracy has impliedly authorized the other to do these acts and to say these things. This exception is not limited to charges of conspiracy but is also applicable to any offence committed pursuant to some common design. The exception is also not limited to criminal conspiracies.[39]

One can immediately discern a problem. The preliminary condition of admissibility, the fact of a conspiracy, is also the very thing sought to be established. Our courts have devised a solution. First, the acts and statements made and said in furtherance of the conspiracy are received into evidence. At the end of the trial, the trier of fact is advised to consider all the evidence and satisfy itself beyond a reasonable doubt that the conspiracy alleged in

---

35 *Rudzinski v. Warner Theatres Inc.*, 114 N.W. 2d 466 at 471 (1962).
36 See *R. v. Strand Electric, supra*, note 26, *per* Laskin J.
37 *Morrison-Knudsen Co. v. British Columbia Hydro & Power Authority* (1973), 36 D.L.R. (3d) 95 (B.C. S.C.).
38 See *Strand Electric, supra*, note 34, *per* Laskin J.
39 See, *e.g., Great West Uranium Mines Ltd. v. Rock Hill Uranium Mines Ltd.*, [1955] 4 D.L.R. 307 (Sask. C.A.).

fact existed. If the conspiracy is found to exist, the trier is advised to consider all the evidence directly admissible against the accused and decide whether, on a balance of probabilities, the accused was a member of the conspiracy. If the trier is satisfied on a balance of probabilities that the accused was a member of the conspiracy, then the trier may make use of the evidence of the acts and statements of the co-conspirators to determine whether it is satisfied beyond a reasonable doubt as to the accused's membership.[40]

Observe the result. During the trial, all the evidence of statements made during the conspiracy is received. The jury is then told at the end of the day that these statements are receivable against the accused if they follow the above formula. One can only speculate as to whether the jury will be able to follow the limiting instructions. There was a constitutional attack on the process but it was not successful.[41]

5. Exceptions Where Declarant Is Unavailable

(a) Declarations Against Interest

The common law recognized an exception to the hearsay rule for a declaration made by a person concerning a matter within his personal knowledge which declaration when made was known to the declarant to be to the declarant's prejudice. The theory was that a person would not say something falsely as to which he knew the truth if the statement was against his own interest. There are grounds of necessity since the declarant is unavailable. It is well to distinguish this from an admission. A declaration against interest is not made by a party.

In the beginning, the prejudice was restricted to adverse effects to the declarant's pecuniary or proprietary interest. More recently, the courts have expanded its use to instances where the declarant's penal interest was adversely affected. It was decided that a declarant who exposed himself to criminal liability was as unlikely to be falsifying as was one who made a declaration against his pecuniary interest.[42] Nevertheless, our courts are clearly suspicious of such declarations. In *Demeter*,[43] the accused had been

---

40   *R. v. Carter*, [1982] 1 S.C.R. 938; and *R. v. Barrow*, [1987] 2 S.C.R. 694. For instruction on how the theory works with a two person conspiracy, see *R. v. Viandante* (1995), 40 C.R. (4th) 353 (Man. C.A.), leave to appeal refused (1996), 115 Man. R. (2d) 160 (note) (S.C.C.).

41   *R. v. Duff* (1994), 32 C.R. (4th) 153 (Man. C.A.). Consider whether the co-conspirator exception fits with the principled approach. See and compare *R. v. Duncan* (2002), 1 C.R. (6th) 265 (Man. Prov. Ct.) and *R. v. Lukacko* (2002), 1 C.R. (6th) 309 (Ont. C.A.).

42   *R. v. O'Brien* (1977), 76 D.L.R. (3d) 513 (S.C.C.); and *R. v. Demeter*, [1978] 1 S.C.R. 538.

43   *Ibid.*

convicted of murder. On appeal, the issue concerned the admissibility of an alleged confession by a deceased declarant. The Court decided that there was nothing in the evidence to show that when the declarant made the statement it was contrary to his interest either penal or pecuniary. At the time of the statement, the declarant was an escaped convict under sentence of life imprisonment. In the result, he could not be sentenced to a consecutive sentence so that there could be no penal consequence for the crime admitted to which he was vulnerable. The Court approved the guidelines for the operation of this exception that had been set out in the Court below:

1. The declaration would have to be made to such a person and in such circumstances that the declarant should have apprehended a vulnerability to penal consequences as a result.
2. The vulnerability to penal consequences would have to be not remote.
3. The declaration must be considered in its totality and if upon the whole tenor the weight is in favour of the declarant, it is not against his interest.
4. In a doubtful case, a court might properly consider whether or not there are other circumstances connecting the declarant with the crime and whether or not there is any connection between the declarant and the accused.
5. The declarant would have to be unavailable by reason of death, insanity, grave illness which prevents the giving of testimony even from a bed, or absence in a jurisdiction to which none of the processes of the court extends.

(b) Dying Declarations

At common law, a deceased's declaration regarding the cause of his death, such declaration founded on declarant's personal knowledge, was receivable in a prosecution for his death provided there was evidence that when he made the declaration he entertained a settled and hopeless expectation of death.[44] The theory is that a person in such an extreme state would not tell a falsehood, quieting the danger of sincerity, and that since the statement is limited to the cause of his death his statement was likely accurate. The limitation to its use in criminal prosecutions is odd. Given the quieting of the hearsay dangers, one would have assumed the exception would be available in all cases, civil and criminal. In the beginning, the exception was not so limited and the limitation, created in the nineteenth

---

44 *Accord*, ss. 30(10) and (11) of the *Canada Evidence Act*. For provincial and territorial provisions dealing with business records, see: R.S.B.C. 1996, c. 124, s. 42; R.S.M. 1987, c. E150, s. 40; R.S.N.B. 1973, c. E-11, ss 49 and 51; R.S.N.W.T. 1988, c. e-8, s. 47; R.S.N.S. 1989, c. 154, s. 23; R.S.P.E.I. 1988, c. E-11, s. 32; R.S.S. 1978, c. S-16, s. 31; R.S.Y. 1986, c. 57, s. 37.

century, was by accident. One might now argue for the reception of such a statement in other cases based on the new discretionary approach.

As an illustration of how the old exceptions are strictly construed in comparison to the new discretionary approach, consider the recent case of *Kharsekin*.[45] The accused was charged with murder. The victim died of a stab wound. Around 1 a.m., the victim, bleeding profusely, appeared at the medical centre. The doctor asked him who had wounded him. The victim said it was the accused. Just after this statement, the victim became unconscious. About 15 to 20 minutes later he was revived. The doctor asked the victim whether his assailant was the accused and the victim nodded his head in agreement. The victim died just before 3:00 a.m. The statements were tendered as dying declarations. The trial judge decided that there was no evidence of a settled hopeless expectation of death and refused to admit. That finding was not challenged on appeal. The Court of Appeal decided that the statements were receivable under *Khan/Smith* and that the trial judge was wrong when he concluded that the indicia of reliablity under that doctrine should be the same as those for dying declarations.

(c) Declarations in the Course of Duty

(i) *Common Law*

At common law, declarations of a deceased person were receivable if the person was under a duty to act, the declarations described the deceased's own activities in carrying out that duty, were made contemporaneously with the activity, and the deceased was then under a duty to record the same. The fact that the declaration was about the declarant's own activities quieted perception dangers, that they were made contemporaneously with the doing of the act quieted memory dangers and the duty to record and the routine nature of the declaration ensured accuracy and stilled any concerns as to sincerity.

The requirement that the declarant be deceased has now been eliminated. In *Ares v. Venner*,[46] the plaintiff had been injured in a skiing accident. The fracture was set by the defendant doctor and a cast applied. The cast was evidently applied too tightly and there was consequent impairment of the plaintiff's circulatory system. In the civil suit, the plaintiff sought to prove negligence by proving that the signs of impairment were manifest and that the doctor should have done something to relieve the pressure. The plaintiff tendered the nurses's notes recording their observations. These notes described the plaintiff's toes as "blue", "bluish pink" and "cold", this

---

45 *R. v. Kharsekin* (1994), 88 C.C.C. (3d) 193 (Nfld. C.A.).
46 *Ares v. Venner*, [1970] S.C.R. 608.

despite the fact the nurses were present in the courtroom and this common law exception needed evidence that the declarant was deceased. The Supreme Court decided that hospital records, including nurses's notes, which were made contemporaneously, by one with personal knowledge and under a duty to record, were receivable as proof of the facts stated therein. For the Court those parameters gave assurances of trustworthiness. The nurses were trained observers, they made the notes contemporaneously with their observations and their duty to keep accurate records was subject to supervision. Thus the dangers of perception, memory and sincerity were minimized. But what of the requirement of necessity? The nurses were alive and well and sitting in the courtroom! For necessity, the Court decided it was to be found in the otherwise serious interference with the convenience of hospital management. The language chosen by the Court in *Ares v. Venner* in concluding its judgment was specific to the fact situation before it and referred to hospital records; the language in the rest of the judgment indicated an invitation to the profession to reform the hearsay rule with a discretionary approach. As we saw above, it took another 20 years for this to happen.

(ii) Business Records Legislation

The federal Legislature and the provincial legislatures recognized that modern business methods were not sufficiently accommodated by the common law and thus statutory provisions have now been enacted. Interestingly the legislatures acted at about the same time that the common law was being developed in *Ares v. Venner*. There is authority that one can use either approach.[47] It deserves mention that while the statutory provisions speak of writings and records the common law exception would also embrace oral statements.

The legislative provisions recognize that there are circumstantial guarantees of accuracy resident in the business context from records which are relied on in the day-to-day carrying out of business activities and which are subject to frequent routine checking. Typically these provisions require that the records be of a kind that are made in the usual and ordinary course of business and that the proponent of the evidence give notice to the other side of their intention to introduce business records into evidence. The legislation

---

47 See *R. v. Monkhouse* (1987), 61 C.R. (3d) 343 (Alta. C.A.) approving the application of *Ares v. Venner* to business records in a criminal case and receiving at common law where the Crown had failed to give the notice required by statute. See also *Setak Computer Services Corp. v. Burroughs Business Machines Ltd.* (1977), 76 D.L.R. (3d) 641 at 646 (Ont. H.C.) applying *Ares v. Venner* to business records in a civil case. *Accord, Tecoglas Inc. v. Domglas Inc.* (1985), 51 O.R. (2d) 196 (H.C.). But compare *Exhibitors Inc. v. Allen* (1989), 70 O.R. (2d) 103 (H.C.).

is quite detailed and the following extracts from the Ontario *Evidence* Act,[48] with references to the counterpart provisions in the *Canada Evidence* Act, serve as an example:

35.—(1) In this section,

"business" includes every kind of business, profession, occupation, calling, operation or activity, whether carried on for profit or otherwise;

"record" includes any information that is recorded or stored by means of any device.[49]

(2) Any writing or record made of any act, transaction, occurrence or event is admissible as evidence of such act, transaction, occurrence or event if made in the usual and ordinary course of any business and if it was in the usual and ordinary course of such business to make such writing or record at the time of such act, transaction, occurrence or event or within a reasonable time thereafter.[50]

(3) Subsection (2) does not apply unless the party tendering the writing or record has given at least seven days' notice of the party's intention to all other parties in the action, and any party to the action is entitled to obtain from the person who has possession thereof production for inspection of the writing or record within five days after giving notice to produce the same.[51]

(4) The circumstances of the making of such a writing or record, including lack of personal knowledge by the maker, may be shown to affect its weight, but such circumstances do not affect its admissibility.

(5) Nothing in this section affects the admissibility of any evidence that would be admissible apart from this section or makes admissible any writing or record that is privileged.[52]

Although the language in the legislation is broad, some judicial interpretations have been quite narrow. In *Adderley*,[53] one of the first decisions interpreting the new legislation, the Court was dealing with hospital records. The record contained a diagnosis. The Court decided that a diagnosis, a professional opinion, was not an act, transaction, occurrence or event within

---

48 R.S.O. 1990, c. E.23.
49 Similar broad definitions of "business" and "record" appear in s. 30(12) of the *Canada Evidence Act*, R.S.C. 1985, c. C-5.
50 *Accord*, s. 30(1) of the *Canada Evidence Act*.
51 *Accord*, s. 30(7) of the *Canada Evidence Act*.
52 *Accord*, ss. 30(10) and (11) of the *Canada Evidence Act*. For provincial and territorial provisions dealing with business records, see: R.S.B.C. 1996, c. 124, s. 42; R.S.M. 1987, c. E.150, s. 49; R.S.N.B. 1973, c. E-11, ss. 49 and 51; R.S.N.W.T. 1988, c. E-8, s. 47; R.S.N.S. 1989, c. 154, s. 23; R.S.P.E.I. 1988, c. E-11, s. 32; R.S.S. 1978, c. S-16, s. 31; R.S.Y. 1986, c. 57, s. 37.
53 *Adderley v. Bremner*, [1968] 1 O.R. 621 (H.C.).

the meaning of those words in the section. Recall that the hospital records in *Ares v. Venner* were opinions: toes were described as "blue", "bluish pink" and "cold". Also in *Adderley*, the Court decided that the hospital record of the patient's history, taken on the patient's admission to hospital, could not be received, this despite the express statement in the legislation that "lack of personal knowledge by the maker, may be shown to affect its weight, but such circumstances do not affect its admissibility." Compare *Grimba*,[54] in which case the Crown sought to prove that the accused was actually a man named "Wilder". The Crown's fingerprint expert was prepared to give his opinion that the fingerprints taken from the accused were the same as those on a fingerprint record over the name of "Wilder", drawn from the identification records of the F.B.I. The Crown's expert had not made that fingerprint record and had no personal knowledge of its accuracy but he had been with the Bureau for 11 years and was able to describe how the Bureau served as a reservoir for fingerprints. More in keeping with the spirit of the legislation's attempt at reform, the Court decided that the evidence was admissible. The Court noted that there were circumstantial guarantees of accuracy one would find in a business context from records which are relied on on a daily basis. Such records, the Court said, systematically produced and regularly relied on, should be received even though they contain hearsay.[55]

Federal and provincial legislation have particular provisions dealing with financial records. For example, the *Canada Evidence Act* provides:

> 29. (1) Subject to this section, a copy of any entry in any book or record kept in any financial institution shall in all legal proceedings be admitted in evidence as proof, in the absence of evidence to the contrary, of the entry and of the matters, transactions and accounts therein recorded.

> (2) A copy of an entry in the book or record described in subsection (1) shall not be admitted in evidence under this section unless it is first proved that the book or record was, at the time of the making of the entry, one of the ordinary books or records of the financial institution, that the entry was made in the usual and ordinary course of business, that the book or record is in the custody or control of the financial institution and that the copy is a true copy of it, and such proof may be given by any person employed by the financial institution who has knowledge of the book or record or the manager or accountant of the financial institution, and may be given orally or by affidavit sworn before any commissioner or other person authorized to take affidavits.[56]

---

54 *R. v. Grimba* (1977), 38 C.C.C. (2d) 469 (Ont. Co. Ct.).

55 For recent adoption of this attitude see *R. v. Martin* (1997), 8 C.R. (5th) 246 (Sask. C.A.) and *R. v. Gregoire* (1998), 130 C.C.C. (3d) 65 (Man. C.A.).

56 There are seven other subsections to s. 29. For provincial and territorial provisions dealing with financial records, see: R.S.A. 1980, c. A-21, s. 42; R.S.B.C. 1996, c. 124, ss. 34 and 43; R.S.M. 1987, c. E.150, s. 48; R.S.N.B. 1973, c. E-11, s. 46; R.S.N. 1970, c. 19, *ss.* 1-

(d) Former Testimony

At common law, if a witness had given testimony on oath in a judicial proceeding, and the witness had thereby been open for cross-examination by the other side in that proceeding, and if that witness was not available at a later judicial proceeding, his testimony at the earlier proceeding would be receivable at a later proceeding provided it was tendered against the same party who earlier had the opportunity to cross-examine.[57] Grounds of necessity reside in the witness's unavailability and there are circumstances guaranteeing reliability resident in the oath and the earlier availability of cross-examination. In criminal cases, there is a statutory embodiment of this common law rule in s. 715 of the *Criminal Code:*

(1) Where, at the trial of an accused, a person whose evidence was given at a previous trial on the same charge, or whose evidence was taken in the investigation of the charge against the accused or on the preliminary inquiry into the charge, refuses to be sworn or to give evidence, or if facts are proved on oath from which it can be inferred reasonably that the person

(a) is dead,
(b) has since become and is insane,
(c) is so ill that he is unable to travel or testify, or
(d) is absent from Canada,

and where it is proved that the evidence was taken in the presence of the accused, it may be read as evidence in the proceedings without further proof, unless the accused proves that the accused did not have full opportunity to cross-examine the witness.

(2) Evidence that has been taken on the preliminary inquiry or other investigation of a charge against an accused may be read as evidence in the prosecution of the accused for any other offence on the same proof and in the same manner in all respects, as it might, according to law, be read in the prosecution of the offence with which the accused was charged when the evidence was taken.

(3) For the purposes of this section, where evidence was taken at a previous trial or preliminary hearing or other proceeding in respect of an accused in the absence of the accused, who was absent by reason of having absconded, the accused is deemed to have been present during the taking of the evidence and to have had full opportunity to cross-examine the witness.[58]

7; R.S.N.W.T. 1998, c. E-8, s. 51; R.S.N.S. 1989, c. 154, s. 21; R.S.O. 1990, c. E.23, s. 33; R.S.P.E.I. 1988, c. E-11, s. 30; R.S.S. 1978, c. S-16, s. 28; R.S.Y. 1986, c. 57, s. 43.

57 *Walkerton (Town) v. Erdman* (1894), 23 S.C.R. 352.

58 R.S.C. 1985, c. C-46. For a provincial provision dealing with former testimony, see R.S.N.B. 1973, c. E-11, s. 33.

In *Potvin*,[59] the Supreme Court decided that a trial judge has discretion to reject evidence, although the statutory conditions set out in s. 715 were satisfied, if in her view it would be unfair to receive the same. The Court gave, as an example of unfairness, where the prosecution knew at the time the evidence was initially taken that the witness would not be available to testify at trial and failed to inform the accused so that he could make the best use of his opportunity to cross-examine the witness at the earlier proceeding. Another example of unfairness suggested by the Court would be where the credibility of the missing witness was crucial and the jury had no opportunity to observe the witness's demeanour and so assess the witness's credibility.

6. Exceptions Not Dependent on the Availability of Declarant[60]

(a) Declarations as to Physical Sensation

The common law permitted receipt of declarations as to physical sensations.[61] The common law did not insist on the declarant's unavailability but there was a necessity of sort in the sense that there was no other source of information as to the declarant's well-being. There were seen to be circumstantial guarantees of reliability resident in the fact that the declarant should be able to accurately perceive his own sensations and that the declarations were limited to his then present feelings. Dangers of insincerity were not quieted. The declaration needed to be limited to complaints or expressions as to physical feeling and could not be extended to include narrative as to the cause of the same.[62]

(b) Declarations as to Mental or Emotional State

Since the common law decided to receive declarations as to physical state, it seemed only natural that for the same reasons it would receive declarations as to mental state.

Suppose, for example, that the material issue in the case is whether the declarant was domiciled in Ontario. Suppose, for the purposes of the law of conflict of laws, domicile requires residence plus an intention to make the residence one's home. An out-of-court statement by the declarant — "I plan

---

59 *R. v. Potvin* (1989), 47 C.C.C. (3d) 289 (S.C.C.).

60 Consider the viability of these exceptions under the principled, discretionary approach.

61 *Youlden v. London Guarantee & Accident Co.* (1912), 4 D.L.R. 721 (Ont. H.C.), affirmed (1913), 12 D.L.R. 433 (Ont. C.A.).

62 *Bacon v. Charlton* (1851), 7 Cush. 586, as quoted in 6 Wigmore, *Evidence* (Chad. Rev.), s. 1718.

to make Ontario my home" — is receivable to prove his intent as the hearsay dangers of communication, memory and perception are absent and grounds of necessity exist in the sense that you couldn't get better evidence of the person's intention. In a civil suit against X for alienation of affections, the plaintiff could introduce the wife-declarant's out-of-court statement "I don't love you anymore". This would be receivable to prove the wife-declarant's present state of mind and further the plaintiff's suit against the defendant.

In the examples given the state of mind was a material issue. Suppose the declarant's state of mind is not the material issue but it is relevant to a material issue. For example, in a murder prosecution, evidence of the deceased's statement "I want it all to end!" indicating her intention to commit suicide may be tendered as evidence that she later did take her own life. Evidence of a deceased's statement "I'm going over to Joe's place tonight" may be tendered as evidence that the deceased did go to Joe's place. On the hearsay danger analysis, above, these statements deserve to be received. It is true that the intention manifested by the statement may not in fact have been carried out but that's not a hearsay problem. It's a problem of relevance.[63] The statement is hearsay evidence of the declarant's then state of mind and the then state of mind is circumstantial evidence from which a trier may infer that the speaker later acted in conformity with his expressed intention.

The accused, Tom, is charged with the murder of Dick. According to the police, Harry was the last person to see Dick alive. Harry is prepared to testify that on the day of Dick's death he heard Dick say "I will go to Tom's place tonight.". This statement, a hearsay statement, tendered to prove the declarant's then existing state of mind is direct evidence of that state of mind. The declarant, from his own personal knowledge, was then describing his own mental state. Perception, communication and memory dangers are minimal although the danger of lack of sincerity is not quieted. There is necessity present in the thought that one couldn't have better evidence of the declarant's state of mind. The hearsay exception operates and the evidence is received. A trier of fact may then accept that hearsay evidence and be satisfied that the declarant at the time he spoke intended to go to Tom's place. A trier might then use that evidence as circumstantial evidence that the declarant's state of mind continued to exist over a period of time. From there the trier might infer that the declarant did, that night, go to Tom's place. The declarant's state of mind is relevant to the issue of whether the declarant in fact went to Tom's place. It is not determinative of the issue. Few pieces of evidence are. The trier will look at all the evidence in the

---

63 *R. v. P. (R.)* (1990), 58 C.C.C. (3d) 334 (Ont. H.C.); and *R. v. Jack* (1992), 70 C.C.C. (3d) 67 (Man. C.A.).

case, including the evidence of the declarant's state of mind, and then, based on all the relevant admissible evidence, will come to a decision.[64]

Suppose the declaration as to state of mind was not of an intention to do some act in the future but rather a statement of the declarant's belief as to a past act done. Should such a statement be receivable? Though the distinction may be regarded as tenuous the answer must be no. If such a statement were receivable the hearsay rule would no longer exist. The exception would have swallowed the rule.

Dr. Shepard is charged with the murder of Sally Jones. A witness is prepared to testify that shortly before Sally's death the witness heard Sally say "Dr. Shepard has poisoned me." Suppose this statement was made under such circumstances that it would not qualify as a dying declaration. The statement, however, is a statement as to the declarant's then existing state of mind, *i.e.*, Sally's belief. As above, the hearsay dangers are limited to the same extent, and the same grounds of necessity exist. Nevertheless, it must he rejected as not falling within this exception. The hearsay rule states that an out-of-court statement cannot be received when tendered to prove the truth of the matter stated. If we, pursuant to the instant exception, receive the statement of the declarant's belief regarding Dr. Shepard having poisoned her the hearsay rule would be finished.

Logical? Perhaps not. But we must maintain a distinction between declarations of intention which illuminate the future and declarations of belief that illuminate the past. Otherwise our beloved hearsay rule would be no more.[65]

(c) Spontaneous Statements

If a declaration is made in response to an event, in circumstances of such spontaneity or involvement that one can say that there was no opportunity for the declarant to reflect on what would have been the best thing for him to say, then we are assured that the hearsay danger of sincerity is eliminated. The declaration being contemporaneous with the event to which the statement is relevant the memory danger is also stilled. The common law has traditionally received such a statement although one can imagine that the very spontaneity that quiets sincerity and memory may cause misperception. Who hasn't said, after an exclamation about some stirring event, "On second thought . . .".[66]

64　In *R. v. Starr* (2000), 36 C.R. (5th) 1 (S.C.C.) the statement, though reflecting a state of mind, intention, was rejected as not in accord with the principled approach as the court saw a motive in the declarant to falsify.

65　*Shepard v. U.S.*, 290 U.S. 96 (1933), *per* Cardozo J.

66　Should this concern regarding perception cause second thoughts regarding the continued existence of this exception pursuant to the principled approach?

This exception was formerly referred to by most, and is still referred to by some, as the *res gesta* exception. That Latin phrase led to considerable confusion and describing it in terms of its underlying rationale, spontaneous declaration, is a marked improvement.[67] The statement need not be contemporaneous with the event as long as it was made while the declarant was still dominated by the event.[68] In *Clark*,[69] the accused was charged with murder. Shortly after she had been injured by the accused the victim yelled "Help, I've been murdered, I've been stabbed." The Court decided that these statements were made spontaneously in circumstances where concoction or distortion could safely be excluded and were therefore admissible. The Court specifically said that the narrow test of exact contemporaneity was no longer to be followed. In *Khan*,[70] the accused was charged with sexual assault. The Crown had sought to introduce statements made by the child to her mother some 15 minutes after the alleged assault, arguing that they were admissible under the spontaneous declaration exception to the hearsay rule. The trial judge refused to admit the statements. The Court of Appeal found that the trial judge had erred in not allowing greater latitude with respect to the lapse of time between the event and the declaration. The Supreme Court decided that the trial judge correctly rejected the mother's statement applying the traditional tests for spontaneous declarations. The Court decided that the statement was not contemporaneous, being made 15 minutes after leaving the doctor's office and probably one-half hour after the offence was committed, and that it was not made under pressure or emotional intensity which would give the guarantee of reliability upon which the spontaneous declaration exception had traditionally rested.[71]

(d) Statements of Present Sense Impression

The common law has received, often with the label *res gesta*, declarations of a present sense of belief concerning a contemporaneous event witnessed by the declarant.[72] To qualify there need not be a startling event or excitement in the declarant. There is spontaneity, however, and the statement does describe a current event. The statement was made in the presence of another, who is now prepared to relate the statement, and that other had an opportunity to see what the declarant saw, and is now open to

---

67 *Ratten v. R.* (1971), [1972] A.C. 378 (Aust. P.C.).
68 *R. v. Andrews*, [1987] A.C. 281 (H.L.).
69 *R. v. Clark* (1983), 42 O.R. (2d) 609 (C.A.).
70 *Supra*, note 11.
71 In the result, the Court received the statements pursuant to the principled discretionary approach described above.
72 *R. v. Graham* (1972), 7 C.C.C. (2d) 93 (S.C.C.).

cross-examination as to the statement and the circumstances surrounding its making.

7. Exceptions Where Declarant is Available[73]

The existing common law position is that an out-of-court statement does not cease to be hearsay simply because the declarant is present in the witness stand.[74] Although the declarant is presently under oath and subject to cross-examination, the statement when made was not so subject and the orthodox view accordingly rejects its use as substantive evidence. It is thought that the worth of cross-examination lies in its immediacy following the making of the statement. It is not sufficient that the opposite party is able at some future date to test the worth of the statement.[75]

In *B. (K.G.)*,[76] the accused and three of his young friends were involved in a fight with two men. During the course of the fight, one of the youths pulled a knife and stabbed one of the men in the chest and killed him. The accused's friends were interviewed by the police and they told the police that the accused had made statements to them in which he acknowledged that he thought he had caused the death of the victim by the use of a knife. The accused was charged with murder. At trial, the three youths recanted their earlier statements and said they had lied to the police. Although the trial judge had no doubt that the recantations were false, the witnesses's prior inconsistent statements could not be tendered as proof that the accused actually made the admissions. Under the traditional common law position, these statements, though the Court was satisfied that they had been earlier made by the young people who were now in the witness stand, could not be used for their truth but could only be used to impeach the witnesses's credibility. The Supreme Court decided in this case that it could apply the principled, discretionary *Khan/Smith* approach to the facts of its case and that the statements could be given truth bearing quality. Without such exceptional treatment the orthodox view would have denied receipt for truth though the declarants were in the stand.

(a) Previous Identification

If a witness has previously identified the accused out-of-court, that fact may be received in evidence at trial to confirm the witness's identification

---

73 Consider the viability of these exceptions under the principled, discretionary approach.
74 See *R. v. Deacon*, [1947] 3 D.L.R. 772 (S.C.C.); and *Lizotte v. R.*, [1951] 2 D.L.R. 754 (S.C.C.).
75 See *State v. Saporen*, 285 N.W. 898 at 901 (1939).
76 *R. v. B. (K.G.)*, *supra*, note 16.

at trial. The dock identification, the statement made at the trial, is supported by the fact of the earlier identification. If the witness is unable to identify the accused at trial, there is no present statement to confirm, and receiving the earlier statement for its truth would violate the hearsay rule since that statement of identification was not made under oath nor then subject to cross-examination. However, there are grounds of necessity resident in the witness's present inability to describe the malefactor and there are sufficient circumstances to guarantee reliability. The accused at trial will be able to cross-examine the eye-witness with regard to his usual powers of perception and memory, and also his sincerity, and will also be able to cross-examine the eye-witness about the circumstances and fairness of the procedure used to conduct the out-of-court identification. The accused will also be able to cross-examine the witness who comes to court to testify that it was the accused before the court who was earlier identified by the eye-witness. Again the circumstances of the earlier identification can be gone into through this witness. These protective safeguards have been found sufficient to warrant receipt of the earlier identification as an exception to the hearsay rule.[77]

(b) Past Recollection Recorded

As we saw in Chapter 3, a witness may testify to a past event having reference to his earlier notes concerning the matter, though he has no present recollection of the event. This is justified on the basis that the adversary will be able to cross-examine the witness regarding his usual habits for accuracy in perception and in recording any motives for falsifying. The contemporaneity of note-taking required for the exercise also gives added assurance of the trustworthiness of the earlier statement. This process, which we describe as refreshment of memory, masks the reception of the earlier hearsay statement but the exception to the rule deserves notice.[78]

---

77 *R. v. Langille* (1990), 59 C.C.C. (3d) 544 (Ont. C.A.); *R. v. Power* (1987), 67 Nfld. & P.E.I.R. 272 (Nfld. T.D.); and *R. v. Skipper* (1988), 69 Sask. R. 7 (Q.B.). In *R. v. Tat* (1997), 14 C.R. (5th) 116 (Ont. C.A.) the court decided the previous identification was not hearsay; for criticism see accompanying Annotation by Delisle.
78 See *R. v. Meddoui* (1990), 61 C.C.C. (3d) 345 (Alta. C.A.), leave to appeal to S.C.C. quashed for want of jurisdiction (1991), 69 C.C.C. (3d) vi (note) (S.C.C.).

5

Opinion and Expert Evidence

1. The Opinion Rule and Lay Witnesses

Two hundred years ago, witnesses were admonished to speak facts and not opinion. This led, in the minds of some, to the creation of a supposed rule forbidding opinion testimony from a lay witness. Closer examination, however, reveals that it was never the intention of the courts to absolutely bar the expression of opinion testimony. When the rule was first announced the word "opinion" had a distinct meaning. It referred to a person's persuasion as to an event, such person being without knowledge. What was being foreclosed was testimony by witnesses who had no personal knowledge of the event and so suffered from the same lack of testimonial qualification as the witness who repeated hearsay. What was forbidden were notions, guesses and conjectures. The courts were not forbidding testimony regarding reasoned conclusions from facts observed.

While we sometimes still read statements that lay witnesses cannot give their opinions but must state facts, think about the intrinsic impossibility of such a requirement.[1] When a witness speaks, facts cannot come out of his mouth. When the witness relates what he saw or heard, he is providing not facts, but rather statements about facts. A statement about a fact is a conclusion that the witness has reached about what he believes he then saw and heard. It is an opinion.[2] The intrinsic impossibility of speaking otherwise led courts to create exceptions to the supposed rule permitting lay witnesses to express their opinion on matters such as the identity of an individual, the apparent age of a person, or the speed of a vehicle.[3] This approach, a rule plus exceptions, accommodated most instances.

Nevertheless, it might be better to see the rule for what it is. It is not an absolute rule of exclusion. It is rather a preferential rule asking the witness to be as precise as possible in his or her opinion as to what he or she saw or heard. For example, it is not helpful to the trier of fact for the witness to say

---

1   See generally King & Pillinger, *Opinion Evidence in Illinois* (1942).

2   *R. v. Miller* (1959), 29 W.W.R. 124 (B.C. C.A.).

3   *R. v. German*, [1947] O.R. 395 (C.A.).

"In my opinion the driver was negligent" or "In my opinion the driver was driving too fast considering the circumstances at the time." Those are questions of fact for the trier to decide. On the other hand, it would be helpful if the witness gave his estimate of the driver's speed, what basis he had for estimating that speed, his best description of the weather at the time and the road conditions. These expressions of estimate and description, are, of course, on reflection, expressions of opinion but that is all that the witness can do. A better formulation of the supposed rule, preferable to a rule plus exceptions, would provide that lay opinions are prohibited, in the discretion of the trial judge, when such an opinion is not helpful to the trier of fact; the corollary, of course, is that helpful opinions from lay witnesses with personal knowledge are receivable.

In *Miller*,[4] the accused was charged with shooting with intent to wound. The victim was prepared to testify to what he thought or believed the accused's state of mind was at the time of the incident, *i.e.*, whether he believed that the accused was intending to wound him or simply to scare him. The Crown objected on the basis that this would be opinion and not fact. The Court, denying the Crown's argument, noted that when a witness testifies that he saw or heard something he is really saying that he thinks or believes he saw or heard what he then describes. It's all a matter of judgment. The Court said that all a witness can do is say what he thinks or believes although the witness seldom prefaces the statement with "I think" or "I believe".

In *Graat*,[5] the accused was convicted of impaired driving. On appeal, it was argued that the trial judge had erred in permitting the arresting officer and the booking sergeant to give their opinion as to whether the accused's ability to operate a motor vehicle was impaired by the use of alcohol. The Court of Appeal dismissed the appeal on the basis that the opinion was admissible as an exception since it was really a compendious mode of giving evidence as to certain facts, in this case the condition of the accused. The Supreme Court also dismissed the appeal but took a very different approach. The Court noted that previous decisions had proceeded on the basis of a supposed rule with a list of exceptions. But the Court said there was little, if any, virtue in any distinction resting on the tenuous and frequently false antithesis between fact and opinion, and preferred to address the problem by looking first at principles. The impugned evidence was regarded by the Court as relevant to a material issue. The officers had observed the accused. Based on their personal observations as to the manner of driving and indicia of intoxication they concluded that his ability to drive was impaired. The

---

4   *R. v. Miller, supra*, note 2.
5   *R. v. Graat* (1982), 31 C.R. (3d) 289 (S.C.C.), affirming (1980), 17 C.R. (3d) 55 (Ont. C.A.).

proper approach to the admissibility of this opinion evidence was then to assess the probative value of the opinion against the possible dangers of confusing the issues, misleading the jury, surprising the adversary and excessive consumption of time. The Court decided that the evidence did not unfairly surprise the accused and that adducing the evidence did not require a great deal of time. The Court rejected as unsound historically and in principle any notion that the reception of opinion testimony would usurp the function of the jury. The Court noted that the trial judge was not in as good a position as the officers to judge the accused's impairment and the officers' expression of opinion would be of real help. The judge could accept all, part or none of their evidence. Applying these general basic principles, the Court decided the evidence was properly received.

2. Expert Witnesses

(a) Generally

We normally require witnesses to have personal knowledge concerning the event at issue. Only such persons are regarded as helpful to the trier of fact. The law has long recognized, however, an exception to this general requirement when the witness has qualifications beyond those of the trier of fact. Those qualifications make his opinion helpful. Such a witness is able to provide, through his expertise, assistance to the trier. Helpfulness is key. Only if the subject-matter is beyond the ken of the trier of fact will the expert be permitted to speak. The courts reasoned that sometimes the trier needed expert guidance and therefore when the evidence of experts was necessary it would be received. The first and foremost requirement for expert testimony is that the expert testimony must be helpful.[6]

Originally, when expert advice was necessary the trial judge would summon the expert. The expert would advise the judge who, in turn, would direct the jury respecting the major premise that could be used by it in determining the particular fact situation. With the change to the adversary system, and the parties calling the necessary factual witnesses, it seemed to be a natural development that by the end of the eighteenth century the experts were being called as witnesses by the parties and the trier was called on to assess the worth of the opinions expressed. The role for the trial judge today is not to assess the expert's opinion and direct the jury accordingly but rather to make sure that the expert will in fact be helpful to the jury in

---

6 See *R. v. Abbey*, [1982] 2 S.C.R. 24; and *R. v. Fisher* (1961), 34 C.R. 320 at 342 (Ont. C.A.).

their determinations. Is it necessary to the correct disposal of the litigation? There are several aspects to this determination of helpfulness or necessity.

The trial judge must first determine that the expert has knowledge beyond the ken of the lay person, that the expertise is not commonly shared. In order for expert evidence to be admissible the subject-matter of the inquiry must be such that ordinary people are unlikely to form a correct judgment about it, if unassisted by persons with special knowledge.[7] If the lay person understands the issue as well as the expert, the opinion will be regarded as not helpful. That is why we often see judicial decisions denying receipt of expert opinions on the issue of what a normal or reasonable person would do in the circumstances. It is expected that a lay juror will know that as well as any other. That line, however, can be difficult to draw.

Psychiatric or psychological testimony may be received as expert evidence in those circumstances where the average person may not have sufficient knowledge or experience with human behaviour to draw an appropriate inference from the facts. In *Lavallee*,[8] the accused was charged with murder. The defence was self-defence. For that defence to succeed, the *Criminal Code* requires that the accused acted under reasonable apprehension of death or grievous bodily harm.[9] The accused had been a battered woman in a volatile common law relationship. She killed her partner late one night by shooting him in the back of the head as he left her room. The shooting occurred after an argument where the accused had been physically abused and was taunted with the threat that either she kill him or he would get her. Did she act under *reasonable* apprehension of death or grievous bodily harm? The Court decided it would be difficult for the lay person to comprehend the battered wife syndrome. The average person might think that battered women are not really beaten as badly as they claim, otherwise they would have left the relationship, or that women enjoy being beaten. The Court recognized that each of these stereotypes might adversely affect consideration of a battered woman's claim to have acted in self-defence. The Court decided that expert evidence could assist the jury in dispelling these myths. The expert testimony would provide an explanation as to why the accused did not flee when she perceived her life to be in danger. The expert testimony might also assist the jury in assessing the reasonableness of her belief that killing her batterer was the only way to save her own life. The Court decided, therefore, that it was proper for the psychiatrist to testify

---

7   In *R. v. D. (D.)* (2000), 36 C.R. (5th) 261 (S.C.C.), the Crown called a child psychologist to testify that a child's delay in alleging sexual abuse did not support an inference of falsehood. The court divided on the issue of whether the psychologist's evidence went beyond the ordinary knowledge and expertise of the jury. The majority decided the evidence was not necessary and should not have been admitted.

8   *R. v. Lavallee* (1990), 55 C.C.C. (3d) 97 (S.C.C.).

9   R.S.C. 1985, c. C-46, s. 34.

that in his opinion the accused's shooting of the deceased was the final desperate act of a woman who sincerely believed that she would be killed that night. The expert testimony was properly admitted in order to assist the jury in determining whether the accused had a *reasonable* apprehension of death or grievous bodily harm and believed on *reasonable* grounds that she had no alternative but to shoot.

In determining helpfulness the judge must decide whether the particular witness being tendered as an expert has the necessary qualifications.[10] These qualifications may be demonstrated by formal educational certificates or by practical experience gained over a period of time. The witness will be examined before the judge and the jury. He may also be cross-examined as to his qualifications. Submissions may be made and the judge will decide if the witness has the necessary experiential qualifications. If the witness is found to be wanting the trier will not be misled as the supposed expert will not testify; if accepted as an expert witness the jury will have the advantage of hearing his qualifications and will be better able to assess the weight to be given to his testimony.

In determining helpfulness it is also for the judge to determine the reliability or validity of the science proposed to be elicited. As the judge is the gatekeeper on other matters concerning helpfulness it is also sensible that he as well protect the trier from so-called "junk" science.[11] In *Mohan*,[12] the accused, a practising paediatrician, was charged with sexual assault on four of his female patients. Counsel for the accused sought to call a psychiatrist who would testify that the perpetrator of the offences alleged to have been committed would be one of a limited and unusual group of individuals, and that the accused did not fall within that narrow class because he did not possess the characteristics belonging to that group. The trial judge refused the evidence and the accused was convicted. The Court of Appeal reversed. The Supreme Court of Canada said that the trial judge, in determining the admissibility of expert evidence, was to be guided by the application of the criteria of relevance and helpfulness. After determining that the evidence was logically relevant to a material issue the judge would assess its probative value against its possible prejudicial effect. The Court recognized that the evidence could mislead in the sense that its effect on the trier of fact, particularly a jury, might be out of proportion to its reliability. There is always a danger that expert evidence could be misused and given more weight than it deserves. It might confuse and confound the jury. Will the

---

10 *Preeper v. R.* (1888), 15 S.C.R. 401.
11 See Huber, *Galileo's Revenge: Junk Science in the Courtroom* (Best Books, 1991).
12 *R. v. Mohan* (1994), 29 C.R. (4th) 243 (S.C.C.). For examples of the application of *Mohan,* see *R. v. Olscamp* (1994), 35 C.R. (4th) 37 (Ont. Gen. Div.) and *R. v. Warren* (1995), 35 C.R. (4th) 347 (N.W.T. S.C.).

jury be able to keep an open mind and objectively assess the worth of the evidence? The court needs to be concerned regarding "human fallibility in assessing the proper weight to be given to evidence cloaked under the mystique of science."[13] In the result, in *Mohan* the Court decided that the trial judge was correct to exclude the evidence. There was no material in the record to support the witness's finding that the profile of a pedophile or psychopath had been standardized to the extent that it could be said that it matched the supposed profile of the offender depicted in the charges. The expert's group profiles were not seen as sufficiently reliable to be considered helpful. In the absence of these indicia of reliability, it could not be said that the evidence would be necessary in the sense of usefully clarifying a matter.

In determining the reliability of novel scientific evidence, the United States Supreme Court came to the same conclusion as our Court, and offered some advice to trial judges.[14] Perhaps some of the general observations in the American decision might be useful to counsel in Canada in framing arguments and to trial judges in deciding the matter. The U.S. Court recognized that it would be wrong to demand that the subject of scientific testimony be known to a certainty. To qualify as scientific knowledge, however, an inference or assertion needed to be derived by the scientific method. The trial judge is expected to assess whether the reasoning or methodology underlying the testimony is scientifically valid and whether that reasoning or methodology can properly be applied to the facts in issue. The U.S. Court offered some observations as to how a trial judge might go about his task:

> Whether a theory or technique is scientific knowledge that will assist the trier of fact will [depend on] whether it can be and has been tested . . . [,] whether the theory or technique has been subjected to peer review and publication . . . . The fact of publication, or lack thereof, in a peer-reviewed journal will be a relevant, though not dispositive, consideration . . . . . [T]he court should consider the known or potential rate of error and the existence and maintenance of standards controlling the technique's operation . . . . Finally, "general acceptance" can yet have a bearing.[15]

The trial judge, the gatekeeper, has the obligation to vet each of these requirements of helpfulness. In determining helpfulness the trial judge must always have regard to the potential of expert evidence to distort the fact-finding process and turn it into a trial of experts, and should exclude when that danger is manifest. Trial judges always have the discretion to exclude

---

13 *R. v. Béland*, [1987] 2 S.C.R. 398 at 434, *per* La Forest J. See also *R. v. Melaragni* (1992), 73 C.C.C. (3d) 348 (Ont. Gen. Div.).

14 *Daubert v. Merrell Dow Pharmaceuticals, Inc.*, 113 S.Ct. 2786 (1993).

15 *Ibid.* at 2796-2797.

even relevant evidence when probative value is overcome by the counter-weights of consumption of time, prejudice and confusion.

(b) The Ultimate Issue Rule

It is not infrequent that we hear counsel and judges refer to the supposed problem of a witness speaking to the ultimate issue. The rule is said to be justified on the basis that to allow such an opinion would permit the expert to usurp the jury's function. It is submitted that this is a red herring.[16] Opinion evidence, like any other evidence, can be accepted or rejected by the trier of fact and their role cannot be usurped. It is much better to recognize that in those cases where the evidence was supposedly rejected as in conflict with that rule, the real reason for rejection lay in the lack of helpfulness.[17] If a witness were to testify that in his opinion the defendant was negligent, or guilty, expressions by the witness on issues which are mixed questions of fact and law, that testimony would not be helpful to the trier of fact.[18] Expressions of opinion less than that will also be judged on helpfulness and not on any so-called ultimate issue rule.

In *Lupien*,[19] the accused was charged with gross indecency. A defence psychiatrist was permitted to testify that the accused's personality make-up was such that he could not have formed the requisite mental state for the crime. The majority of the Supreme Court decided that while this evidence came close to the very thing that the jury had to decide, if not identical thereto, this was not a reason to exclude. The weight to be given the opinion was for the jury to decide following appropriate instructions from the trial judge.

In *Cooper*,[20] the accused was charged with murder. In answer to a question put by the trial judge the psychiatrist testified that he did not think that the accused was suffering with a disease of the mind. Nonetheless, the trial judge dealt with this issue of insanity in her charge to the jury. The majority of the Court noted that while the term "disease of the mind" in s. 16 of the *Criminal Code* was a legal concept, and what is meant by the term was a question of law for the judge, as a matter of practice the trial judge could permit the psychiatrist to be asked directly whether or not the condition in question constituted a disease of the mind.

---

16   7 Wigmore, *Evidence* (Chad. Rev.), s. 1921.
17   See *R. v. Fisher, supra,* note 6.
18   See, *e.g., R. v. Neil,* [1957] S.C.R. 685.
19   *R. v. Lupien* (1970), 9 C.R.N.S. 165 (S.C.C.).
20   *Cooper v. R.,* [1980] 1 S.C.R. 1149.

Although appellate decisions have frequently denied the existence of the rule,[21] it continues to be invoked. For example, in *Khan*[22] there had allegedly been a sexual assault on a young girl. The accused was a medical doctor. He was disciplined by his professional body. On appeal to the Divisional Court that body decided, *inter alia*, that the discipline committee had erred in receiving the evidence of two experts to the effect that the child had been sexually abused since that was evidence going to the ultimate issue to be determined by the committee and was beyond the proper scope of expert evidence. The Court of Appeal decided that to exclude the expert's evidence that a certain factual inference should be drawn because that fact is at the core of the dispute would exclude the most probative part of the expert's evidence. The Court recognized that there is a danger when the expert evidence goes to the ultimate issue as the trier might too readily adopt the same. But the Court said the answer is not an automatic exclusion but rather the exercise of the trial judge's discretion to exclude evidence if it is not helpful or if it unfairly prejudices the proper outcome of the trial. If the opinion evidence can be given just as accurately in less conclusory terms the trial judge might insist on that as long as that does not affect its honesty or accuracy.

(c) Hypothetical Questions

When an expert expresses her opinion she bases the same on her knowledge of the applicable science and on the assumption that certain facts specific to the case have teen established. All opinions are then, in a sense, hypothetical.

The expert after being examined as to her credentials will be asked to set out the basis of her opinion. Sometimes the expert will have personally examined the person or object of the opinion and will then set out her observations of the same. At other times the expert will have no personal knowledge and will be basing her opinion on the evidence of others. In either event the trial judge will tell the jury that they must first examine the worth of the evidence concerning the basis for the opinion. If they accept that evidence, are persuaded to the requisite degree that the facts on which the opinion is based actually did exist, they will be advised to go on and determine whether they are persuaded that the opinion ought to be accepted. If they are not persuaded that the facts upon which the opinion is based actually existed the expert's opinion is valueless.

---

21 See, *e.g.*, *R. v. Graat* (1980), 55 C.C.C. (2d) 429 at 443 (Ont. C.A.) where Howland C.J.O. said "the ultimate issue doctrine may now be regarded as having been virtually abandoned or rejected" [affirmed *supra*, note 5].

22 *Khan v. College of Physicians & Surgeons (Ontario)* (1992), 9 O.R. (3d) 641 (C.A.).

If the jury is to adequately assess the worth of an expert opinion it is essential that the basis be clearly set out for them. Often this is done through the technique of hypothetical questions. Suppose the accused is charged with murder. A psychiatrist is called as a witness. "Doctor Smith, we have heard the accused testify as to the facts that occurred on the evening in question. That before the unfortunate occurrence he had consumed 24 pints of beer. That he had had nothing to eat for the previous 24 hours. That he had not had any sleep for the previous 24 hours. That he was not accustomed to taking in large quantities of alcohol. Based on those facts what can you tell us as to the ability of the accused to form the requisite intent to kill?" The doctor then testifies that, in his opinion, based on those facts, and based on his studies and his personal experience with intoxicated persons, the accused lacked the necessary capacity to form the required intent. The trier then has the basis for the opinion clearly set out and will be advised that their first task is to determine whether the basis of the opinion has been established to their satisfaction. The trier will then consider whether the accused's evidence ought to be accepted. If it is not accepted then the opinion must be rejected. If the facts as described are found to exist the trier will go on to determine whether to accept or reject the expert's opinion. The expert's opinion, like any other piece of evidence, is for the trier of fact to accept or reject.

(d) Expert Opinion Based on Hearsay

It is commonly said that an expert is confined to expressions of opinion based on facts proved at the trial. The opinion is then elicited based on the acceptance of those facts as true using the device of hypothetical questions. But an expert testifying to her opinion, since only permitted so to do when she possesses particular knowledge or experience not shared by the trier of fact, frequently relies on hearsay. In developing her expertise she often relied on the statements of her instructors and those of text writers without satisfying herself by personal experiment that their instruction was accurate. It is perfectly acceptable for the expert to rely on the opinions of text writers where those texts are recognized by the profession as authoritative. In cross-examination an expert witness, having first been asked whether a certain textbook is recognized as authoritative by her profession, may have read to her passages from such book expressing another opinion for the purpose of testing the value of the witness's expressed opinion.[23]

So too there is a growing recognition that an expert may be able to give his opinion though it be based partly on hearsay evidence if there are grounds of necessity and reliability. For example, a real estate assessor who is called

---

23 *R. v. Anderson* (1914), 16 D.L.R. 203 at 220 (Alto. C.A.).

on to give his opinion on the value of a piece of property will naturally rely on statements of others, perhaps found in the registry office, as to what other like properties fetched on the market. This is how he regularly goes about his business.[24] There are grounds of necessity: receiving his opinion rather than calling all the persons who sold their houses over a period of time. There are circumstances of reliability resident in the absence of any motive to falsify and in the cumulative nature of the evidence relied on. A psychiatrist asked for an opinion as to an offender's dangerousness will base his opinion not only on his own interviews and tests but will also study the individual's previous records. This is how he normally goes about his tasks.[25] Again we have circumstances of necessity and reliability.

Suppose, however, the hearsay relied on has within it concern as to trustworthiness. What then should we do? In *Lavallee*,[26] the accused was charged with murder. We saw earlier how the psychiatric expert was determined to be valuable in helping the jury decide whether her actions were reasonable. The expert in *Lavallee* based his opinion on his expertise in the area of battered woman syndrome, gained through the literature and his own experience. He also accepted as true information he had received from the accused during four hours of interviews, the police report, an interview with the accused's mother and hospital reports documenting eight of her visits to hospital emergency departments. The accused did not testify. The Crown introduced into evidence the statement she gave to the police on the evening of the shooting. That statement, inculpatory in that it described the shooting, was also exculpatory in that it detailed how frightened she was and how her partner had yelled at and hit her. Our Court, in a most pragmatic exercise, said that insofar as the opinion is based on admissible evidence the fact that it is partly based on hearsay does not impact on admissibility but rather only on weight and the trier is to be so advised. Such advice is admittedly hard to formulate and may be even more difficult to follow. Another solution might be to have the expert testify after all the other witnesses have testified and then the trial judge could ask the expert to testify solely on the basis of the admissible evidence.[27]

(e) Number of Experts

There are statutory limits on the number of expert witnesses that can be called.[28] The legislation provides for more with leave of the court. The

---

24 See *Saint John (City) v. Irving Oil Co.* (1966), 58 D.L.R. (2d) 404 (S.C.C.).

25 See *R. v. Wilband*, [1967] 2 C.C.C. 6 (S.C.C.).

26 *R. v. Lavallee, supra*, note 8.

27 See *Mizzi v. DeBartok* (1992), 9 O.R. (3d) 383 (Gen. Div.).

28 The *Canada Evidence Act*, R.S.C. 1985, c. C-5, limits each party to five: s. 7. By the

Supreme Court decided that this legislation permitted the calling of the number specified with respect to each issue on which expert evidence was necessary as opposed to that number in the whole trial.[29]

3. Exchange of Expert Reports

In the interests of efficiency at trial and to minimize inconvenience to some experts who are regularly called on for their opinions some provinces have enacted legislation. For example, the Ontario *Evidence Act* provides:

52.—(1) In this section,

"practitioner" means,

(a) a member of a College as defined in subsection 1(1) of the *Regulated Health Professions Act, 1991,*
(b) a drugless practitioner registered under the *Drugless Practitioners Act,*
(c) a person licensed or registered to practise in another part of Canada under an Act that is similar to an Act referred to in clause (a) or (b).
(d) [Repealed 1998, c. 18, Sched. G, s. 50.]
(e) [Repealed 1998, c. 18, Sched. G, s. 50.]
(f) [Repealed 1998, c. 18, Sched. G, s. 50.]

(2) A report obtained by or prepared for a party to an action and signed by a practitioner and any other report of the practitioner that relates to the action are, with leave of the court and after at least ten days' notice has been given to all other parties, admissible in evidence in the action.

(3) Unless otherwise ordered by the court, a party to an action is entitled, at the time that notice is given under subsection (2), to a copy of the report together with any other report of the practitioner that relates to the action.

(4) Except by leave of the judge presiding at the trial, a practitioner who signs a report with respect to a party shall not give evidence at the trial unless the report is given to all other parties in accordance with subsection (2).

(5) If a practitioner is required to give evidence in person in an action and the court is of the opinion that the evidence could have been produced as effectively by way of a report, the court may order the party that required the

---

provincial evidence and territorial Acts, the limits are three in Alberta (R.S.A. 1980, c. A-21, s. 10), three in Manitoba (R.S.M. 1987, c. E.150, s. 25), three in New Brunswick (R.S.N.B. 1973, c. E-11, s. 23), five in Nova Scotia (R.S.N.S. 1989, c. 154, s. 48), three in the Northwest Territories (R.S.N.W.T. 1998, c. E-8, s. 9), three in Ontario (R.S.O. 1990, c. E.23, s. 12), five in Saskatchewan (R.S.S. 1978, c. S-16, s. 48) and three in the Yukon Territory (R.S.Y. 1986, c. 57, s. 9).

29 *Ure v. Fagnan,* [1958] S.C.R. 377.

attendance of the practitioner to pay as costs therefor such sum as the court considers appropriate.[30]

---

30 R.S.O. 1990, c. E.23, s. 52, amended by 1998, c. 18. To like effect, see: R.S.S. 1978, c. S-16, s. 32; R.S.M. 1987, c. E.150, s. 50; R.S.P.E.I. 1988, c. E-11, s. 33. See R.S.B.C. 1996, c. 124, ss. 10 and 11, not restricting the scheme to medical experts.

6

Excluding Evidence for Purposes Other Than Truth

1. Introduction

The rules of evidence that we have examined in the earlier Chapters of this book were largely designed to promote an approximation to truth. The rules we are about to examine in this Chapter restrict our search for truth and must therefore be justified by some other value. The public has an interest in the accurate outcome of litigation; to exclude information that would assist in that regard there must be another public interest that can be identified and that can be seen to outweigh the other.

2. Privileged Communications

(a) Solicitor-Client

From the earliest times, the courts have recognized a privilege for communications between a lawyer and his or her client. In the beginning it was seen to be the lawyer's privilege and was founded in notions of honour. It was dishonourable to disclose a communication made in confidence. Later a new basis for the privilege was recognized and the privilege was seen to be that of the client. Our courts recognized that the administration of justice required counsel to assist the litigant. Litigation required professional advice. The litigant could not pursue his remedy or defence unless the litigant could make a clean breast of things to the professional he had engaged.[1] The privilege protects the litigant against the disclosure of any confidential communication made by the litigant to his lawyer and any communications made in response which communications were made while the litigant was

---

1 *Greenough v. Gaskell* (1831), 39 E.R. 618 at 620-621 (Ch. Div.), approved in *Solosky v. Canada* (1979), 50 C.C.C. (2d) 495 at 506 (S.C.C.). See also *Anderson v. Bank of British Columbia* (1876), 2 Ch. Div. 644 (C.A.).

seeking legal advice.[2] The privilege attaches whether or not litigation was then contemplated. The privilege may attach even to the identity of the client if the client intended the same to be confidential.[3] The privilege attaches when the client seeks legal advice — even though the lawyer has not as yet accepted a retainer the privilege is present.[4]

For the communication to be privileged, the client must be seeking legal advice from one who is,[5] or who the client reasonably believes to be,[6] professionally qualified to practice law.[7] On the other hand, the fact that one party to a communication is professionally qualified does not automatically make the communication privileged; it must be legal advice that is being sought.[8] A lawyer engaged by a corporation to give legal advice oftentimes will be called on to work for his employer in another capacity. The character of the particular work performed must be looked at to see whether the privilege attaches.[9]

If the client is seeking advice to assist in the furtherance of a criminal purpose, our courts have said that this cannot be legal advice being sought and therefore communications of such sort are not privileged.[10] To displace the privilege in such a case there must be more than just an allegation — there must be some evidence from which the judge can infer the illegal purpose.[11]

The Supreme Court has recently emphasized that the solicitor-client privilege is not absolute.[12] In certain circumstances other societal values must prevail. Where a solicitor had retained the services of a psychiatrist who determined that the client was a danger to the public safety the privilege would be set aside. The Court created what has become known as the Public Safety Exception to Solicitor-Client Privilege. Also the Court has created another exception: the Innocence at Stake exception. If an accused can establish that it is necessary to make full answer and defence to a criminal charge that a client's communications to his solicitor be disclosed there will be an exception requiring disclosure.[13]

---

2 *Descôteaux v. Mierzwinski* (1982), 70 C.C.C. (2d) 385 (S.C.C.).

3 *Thorson v. Jones* (1973), 38 D.L.R. (3d) 312 (B.C. S.C.).

4 *Descoteaux v. Mierzwinski, supra,* note 2.

5 *United States v. Mammoth Oil Co.,* [1925] 2 D.L.R. 966 (Ont. C.A.).

6 *R. v. Choney* (1908), 17 Man. R. 467 (C.A.).

7 *United States v. Mammoth Oil Co., supra,* note 5.

8 See, *e.g., Alfred Crompton Amusement Machines v. Customs & Excise Commissioners* (No. 2), [1972] 2 All E.R. 353 at 376 (C.A.), *per* Lord Denning.

9 See, *e.g., Canary v. Vested Estates Ltd.,* [1930] 3 D.L.R. 989 (B.C. S.C.).

10 *R. v. Cox* (1884), 14 Q.B.D. 153 at 167, approved in *Solosky v. Canada, supra,* note 1.

11 *Goodman & Carr v. Minister of National Revenue,* [1968] 2 O.R. 814 (H.C.).

12 See *Smith v. Jones* (1999), 22 C.R. (5th) 203 (S.C.C.).

13 See *R. v. McClure* (2001), 40 C.R. (5th) 1 (S.C.C.). But see *R. v. Brown* (2002), 50 C.R. (5th) 1 (S.C.C.) emphasizing that the Innocence at Stake exception allows for breach of

Originally, solicitor-client privilege operated only to permit the lawyer to refuse to answer questions or to produce documents at trial. Traditionally as well, the privilege did not operate to foreclose a third-party witness, such third party not being an agent of the client or the lawyer, disclosing what he had overheard pass between the lawyer and his client.[14] The lawyer and his client were expected to take precautions against being overheard. There has since been a recognition, however, that the privilege may operate at an earlier time. For example, some of our courts allowed that an application to quash a search warrant for a lawyer's office might be made when the purpose of issuing the warrant was to allow the seizure of documents believed to afford evidence; if such documents attracted a privilege claim they could not very well afford evidence.[15] This led some to suggest that the privilege had become a rule of property rather than just a rule of evidence. While viewing the privilege as a property right bereft of any evidentiary connection was rejected by our Court,[16] there was later recognized to be a substantive right to confidentiality that is broader than the privilege and may be even more protective of the relationship. In *Descoteaux*,[17] a citizen was suspected of lying about his financial means in order to obtain legal aid. This would be a crime. The police gained a search warrant to search the legal aid bureau and seize the form filled out by the citizen at his interview. The seizure was effected and the documents taken were sealed. Descoteaux and the legal aid bureau applied to a judge to have the seizure quashed and the form returned. The Supreme Court decided that it was not necessary to wait for the trial before raising the issue of confidentiality. The Court formulated a substantive rule of confidentiality as follows:

1. The confidentiality of communications between solicitor and client may be raised in any circumstances where such communications are likely to be disclosed without the client's consent.
2. Unless the law provides otherwise, when and to the extent that the legitimate exercise of a right would interfere with another person's right to have his communications with his lawyer kept confidential, the resulting conflict should be resolved in favour of protecting the confidentiality.
3. When the law gives someone the authority to do something which, in the circumstances of the case, might interfere with that confidentiality,

---

solicitor-client privilege only in rare circumstances. For comment see Layton, *R. v. Brown: Protecting Legal-Professional Privilege*, (2002) 50 C.R. (5th) 37.

14 *Lloyd v. Mostyn* (1842), 152 E.R. 558 at 560 (Exch. Ct.); and *Calcraft v. Guest*, [1898] 1 Q.B. 759 at 764 (C.A.).

15 For a list of citations to these cases, see *Solosky v. Canada, supra,* note 1.

16 *Solosky v. Canada, ibid.*

17 *Descoteaux v. Mierzinski, supra,* note 2.

the decision to do so and the choice of means of exercising that authority should be determined with a view to not interfering with it except to the extent absolutely necessary in order to achieve the ends sought by the enabling legislation.

4.   Acts providing otherwise in situations under paragraph 2 and enabling legislation referred to in paragraph 3 must be interpreted restrictively.

The Court sent the matter back for consideration in accordance with these principles. The Court in *Descoteaux* recognized that the rule of evidence did not in any way prevent a third-party witness from introducing into evidence confidential communications made by a client to his lawyer. But the Court said that before allowing such evidence to be introduced the judge must now satisfy himself, through the application of the third substantive rule, that what was being sought to be proved by the communications was important to the outcome of the case and that there was no reasonable alternative form of evidence that could be used for that purpose.

There is now recognition that precautions by the parties may not always be possible and the *Criminal Code* provides that information gained through electronic surveillance that, but for the interception, would have been privileged remains privileged.[18]

(b)   Third Parties and Work Product

Oftentimes it is necessary to the proper conduct of litigation that the lawyer engage the services of a third party to assist. The third party might be his clerical staff, an expert or a private investigator. If litigation is in contemplation when communications to and from these third parties are made, those communications are similarly protected under the umbrella of solicitor-client privilege.[19] If Paul Drake or Della Street gain information about the case while Perry Mason is preparing for trial, that information is privileged from disclosure.

The Americans decided that materials created in anticipation of litigation needed to be protected from disclosure. They labelled these materials the "work product" of the lawyer.[20] In anticipation of litigation, interviews must be conducted, statements taken, memoranda to files written. All these together with counsel's briefs, records of his mental impressions and personal beliefs make up his file. All are necessary to the proper conduct of the litigation. Unless these materials were protected from disclosure the adversary system would break down. In Canada, as well, we have recog-

---

18   R.S.C. 1985 c. C-46, s. 189(6).

19   *Wheeler v. Le Marchant* (1881), 17 Ch. Div. 675 at 682, relied on in *Goodman & Carr v. Minister of National Revenue, supra,* note 11.

20   *Hickman v. Taylor,* 329 U.S. 495 (1947).

nized the correctness of this policy and said material is protected under the umbrella of solicitor-client privilege.[21]

(c) Marital Privilege

When spouses of parties were made competent and compellable witnesses in civil cases in England, the legislation also provided for a privilege with respect to communications between the spouses which communications were made during the marriage. This legislation was copied in Canada. The *Canada Evidence Act*, s. 4, provides:

> 4. (3) No husband is compellable to disclose any communication made to him by his wife during their marriage, and no wife is compellable to disclose any communication made to her by her husband during their marriage.[22]

It is important to note that although the spouse may be a competent and compellable witness in certain criminal cases, this fact does not affect the privilege to refuse to answer questions regarding marital communications.[23] It is noteworthy that this privilege, unlike the solicitor-client privilege, belongs, mysteriously, not to the communicant but to the recipient of the communication.

Does communication refer only to statements made or does it also cover acts and facts discovered during the relationship? In *Gosselin*,[24] the accused was charged with murder. The wife, over objection, was forced to disclose the fact that she had discovered her husband's clothes with bloodstains shortly after the incident. The Supreme Court decided this was not a "communication" within the meaning of the legislation.

The legislation speaks of no husband or wife being obliged to disclose. By definition then, a widow(er) or divorced person cannot claim this privilege.[25]

The privilege allows the spouse to refuse to disclose. That is the essence of the privilege. At common law, the privilege did not foreclose a third-party witness from disclosing what the third party had overheard. In *Rump-*

---

21 *Ottawa-Carleton (Regional Municipality) v. Consumers' Gas Co.* (1990), 74 O.R. (2d) 637 at 643 (Div. Ct.). But see the Public Safety Exception, *supra*.
22 R.S.C. 1985, c. C-5. For similar provincial and territorial provisions, see: R.S.A. 2000, c. A-18, s. 8; R.S.B.C. 1996, c. 124, s. 8; R.S.M. 1987, c. E150, s. 8; R.S.N.B. 1973, c. E-11, s. 10; R.S.N.L. 1990, c. E-16, s. 4; R.S.N.W.T. 1988, c. E-8, s. 4; R.S.N.S. 1989, c. 154, s. 49; R.S.O. 1990, c. E.23, s. 11; R.S.P.E.l. 1988, c. E-11, s. 9; R.S.S. 1978, c. S-16, s. 36; and R.S.Y. 1986, c. 57, s. 6.
23 See *R. v. Zylstra* (1995), 41 C.R. (4th) 130 (Ont. C.A.); and *R. v. Jean* (1979), 7 C.R. (3d) 338 (Alta. C.A.). See *contra, R. v. St. Jean* (1976), 32 C.C.C. (2d) 438 (Que. C.A.).
24 *Gosselin v. R.* (1903), 33 S.C.R. 255.
25 *Shenton v. Tyler*, [1939] 1 Ch. 620 (C.A.); and *R. v. Kanester*, [1966] 4 C.C.C. 231 at 240 (B.C. C.A.) applying *Shenton v. Tyler*.

ing,[26] the accused was charged with murder. The accused, about to set sail, had given a letter to a fellow seaman to post. The letter, to the accused's wife, amounted to a confession. Instead of posting the letter it was turned over to the police. The House of Lords decided the legislation in its terms did not prevent proof of the communication; the legislation only bestowed a privilege in the spouse not to answer questions about the communication.[27] The third parties are expected to take the necessary precautions.

The *Criminal Code*, dealing with invasion of privacy and elecromagnetic interception of private communications, provides:

> Any information obtained by an interception that, but for the interception, would have been privileged remains privileged and inadmissible as evidence without the consent of the person enjoying the privilege.[28]

In *Lloyd*,[29] the accused, husband and wife, were charged with conspiracy to traffic in narcotics. Pursuant to lawful authority, telephone conversations between them were intercepted and introduced into evidence. The Court of Appeal, basing itself on the time-honoured tradition described above, said that while there was a privilege in a spouse to refuse to divulge the information conveyed the information itself was not privileged. The Supreme Court decided that, in order to make some sense of the *Criminal Code* provision, notwithstanding the tradition, the communications were privileged.[30]

(d) Privilege for Without Prejudice Communications

There is a public interest in the settlement of disputes.[31] If all legal disputes went to trial, our courts could not handle the workload and so our law encourages litigants to settle their differences by privileging their communications when they were made in an attempt to settle. The communications of offers to settle at a certain amount might be viewed as conduct amounting to an admission of fault and, without the privilege, be receivable in the subsequent suit.

When parties try to settle a dispute they will often label their communications to be "without prejudice". Whether labelled as "without prejudice" or not, such communications are held to be privileged if, objectively viewed,

---

26 *Rumping v. Director of Public Prosecutions*, [1962] 3 All E.R. 256 (H.L.).
27 *Accord, R. v. Kotapski* (1981), 66 C.C.C. (2d) 78 (Que. S.C.).
28 Section 189(6).
29 *R. v. Lloyd* (1981), 64 C.C.C. (2d) 169 (S.C.C.).
30 Interestingly nothing was said as to whether communications in furtherance of a crime should be excepted.
31 See *Middelkamp v. Fraser Valley Real Estate Board* (1992), 71 B.C.L.R. (2d) 276 (C.A.); and *Rush and Tompkins v. Greater London Council*, [1989] A.C. 1280 (H.L.).

the communications were meant to come to an agreement regarding the matter. The application of the rule is not dependent on the use of the phrase.[32]

The privilege operates, not only with respect to the parties who entered into the negotiations, but also with respect to third parties. In *Waxman*,[33] there had been an attempt to settle a dispute between two parties. Waxman had purchased a hydraulic press from United Steel. This machine was used for the purpose of crushing old motor-cars. The fluid used in the machine was a special kind of oil made by Texaco. An explosion occurred. Waxman sued United Steel and also sued Texaco. Letters had been written between Waxman and United Steel. These letters were marked as being written without prejudice and their contents related to settlement negotiations between them. The Court decided that a party to a correspondence within the without prejudice privilege is protected from being required to disclose it on discovery or at trial in proceedings by or against a third party. The Court reasoned that, as the privilege was intended to encourage amicable settlements and to protect parties to negotiations for that purpose, it was in the public interest that it not be given a restrictive application.

Public policy also encourages compromise in criminal cases. If the vast majority of criminal cases was not settled by a guilty plea the system of criminal justice would grind to a halt. That policy should similarly then protect from disclosure admissions of culpability made by an accused to the Crown if engaged in plea bargaining.[34] The public has as much an interest in encouraging the settlement of criminal cases as it has in civil. In *Draskovic*,[35] the accused, while in the prisoner's dock, motioned to one of the investigating officers to come over to the dock and said that he would plead guilty to five charges if a charge of armed robbery was dropped. The officer testified that he replied that they would proceed on all charges. Evidence of the conversation was admitted by the trial judge. The Court of Appeal decided that it was not necessary to decide whether there existed in Canada any privilege with respect to discussions between counsel for the accused and counsel for the Crown with respect to what charges will be proceeded with and what pleas will be made. The Court decided that what had occurred was not plea bargaining but was simply a voluntary statement made by the accused to the detective who had no authority to do anything other than report the making of the statement to someone else. While statements between counsel engaged in legitimate plea bargaining should be privileged,

---

32 See *Travelers Indemnity Co. of Canada v. Maracle* (1991), 80 D.L.R. (4th) 652 at 658 (S.C.C.).

33 *I. Waxman & Sons Ltd. v. Texaco Canada Ltd.* (1968), 67 D.L.R. (2d) 295 (Ont. H.C.), affirmed [1968] 2 O.R. 452 (C.A.).

34 Describing the American approach to this effect, see *McCormick on Evidence,* 4th ed. (St. Paul: West Publishing, 1992), c. 25, para. 266, at 198.

35 *R. v. Draskovic* (1971), 5 C.C.C. (2d) 186 (Ont. C.A.).

statements made by an accused to a victim should perhaps be dealt with differently. Such statements might be seen to encompass buying off the prosecuting witness or compounding the crime and should not be privileged.[36]

(e) Crown Privilege — Public Interest Immunity

In a suit between private parties, or in a suit by a private party against the government, when production of a government document is sought, the government might resist production on the grounds that production of such a document would be injurious to the public interest. This claim of immunity from disclosure was normally called a claim of Crown Privilege. More recently this phrase has been described as inapt and the same is now referred to by some as a claim for public interest immunity.[37] Some continue using the older phrase.[38]

The claim may be made for different reasons. For example, in a civil suit for damages against a shipbuilder, where the plaintiff sought production of the plans for the ship, production was resisted on the basis that disclosure of the contents of the requested document would hurt the war effort by disclosing to the enemy military secrets.[39] This would be seen as a "contents" claim to Crown privilege. In other circumstances the claim might be on the basis that while the particular document had no information the disclosure of which would be injurious to the public interest, the document belonged to a class of documents that needed to be kept confidential in order to promote candour and completeness of communication. For example, it is necessary for the proper conduct of government affairs that documents disclosing the minutes of Cabinet meetings be kept confidential. This sort of claim would be characterized as a "class" claim to Crown privilege.[40]

Claims of Crown privilege are normally made by the filing of a ministerial certificate with the court. Claims of privilege on the basis of the contents of the document are normally allowed as it would be rare for a court to go beyond a certificate of the responsible member of the executive that it would be contrary to the public interest to make public the contents of a particular document.[41] The courts, however, often say that a claim on the basis of class can be vetted by the judge who can balance the injury to the public interest, resident in the disclosure of such a document, against

---

36 See *R. v. Pabani* (1994), 17 O.R. (3d) 659 (C.A.).
37 *Rogers v. Home Secretary,* [1973] A.C. 388 at 400 (H.L.).
38 See Martland J. in *Canada (Solicitor General) v. Royal Commission Re Health Records* (1982), 62 C.C.C. (2d) 193 at 226 (S.C.C.).
39 *Duncan v. Cammell Laird & Co.,* [1942] A.C. 624 (H.L.).
40 See *Conway v. Rimmer,* [1968] 1 All E.R. 874 (H.L.).
41 See *Goguen v. Gibson* (1983), 10 C.C.C. (3d) 492 (Fed. C.A.).

the injury to the public interest that the administration of justice not be frustrated by the non-disclosure of documents.

Much of the area concerning federal claims is now governed by statute.[41a] The *Canada Evidence Act* provides:

> 37. (1) A minister of the Crown in right of Canada or other official may object to the disclosure of information before a court, person or body with jurisdiction to compel the production of information by certifying orally or in writing to the court, person or body that the information should not be disclosed on the grounds of a specified public interest.

> 39. (1) Where a minister of the Crown or the Clerk of the Privy Council objects to the disclosure of information before a court, person or body with jurisdiction to compel the production of information by certifying in writing that the information constitutes a confidence of the Queen's Privy Council for Canada, disclosure of the information shall be refused without examination or hearing of the information by the court, person or body.

> [Subsections (2)-(4) deal with definitions of Cabinet documents.][42]

Notice that while there is a balancing to be done by the judiciary with respect to most claims of privilege, the claim with respect to the class of documents normally referred to as Cabinet documents is absolute and dependent solely on a member of the executive certifying that the document belongs to that class.[43]

Compare a provincial class claim. In *Carey*,[44] the government of Ontario became increasingly involved with Minaki Lodge, a resort in northwestern Ontario, and eventually became the owner. The previous owner launched a civil suit against the government seeking damages for breach of agreement, deceit and damage to reputation. On examination for discovery the defendant's witnessses claimed absolute privilege respecting all documents that went to or emanated from Cabinet. The Ontario *Evidence* Act provides:

> 30. Where a document is in the official possession, custody or power of a member of the Executive Council, or of the head of a ministry of the public service of Ontario, if the deputy head or other officer of the ministry has the document in his or her personal possession, and is called as a witness, he or she is entitled, acting herein by the direction and on behalf of such member of

---

41a   The *Canada Evidence Act*, ss. 37 and 38 have now been amended by 2001, c. 41, s. 43.

42   For provincial and territorial provisions dealing with Crown privilege, see: R.S.A. 1980, c. A-21; R.S.N.B. 1973, c. E-11, s. 68; R.S.N.W.T. 1988, c. E-8, s. 46; R.S.O. 1990, c. E.23, s. 30; R.S.P.E.I. 1988, c. E-11, s. 29; and R.S.Y. 1986, c. 57, s. 36.

43   *Canada (Attorney General) v. Central Cartage Co.* (1990), 71 D.L.R. (4th) 253 (Fed. C.A.), leave to appeal to S.C.C. refused (1991), 74 D.L.R. (4th) viii (note) (S.C.C.). In this case, the legislative provision withstood Charter challenge as the Court found no violation of s. 15.

44   *Carey v. Ontario*, [1986] 2 S.C.R. 637.

the Executive Council or head of the ministry, to object to producing the document on the ground that it is privileged, and such objection may be taken by him or her in the same manner, and has the same effect, as if such member of the Executive Council or head of the ministry were personally present and made the objection.

The claim in *Carey* was not based on the contents of the documents but on the class to which they belonged. Production, it was claimed, would breach confidentiality and inhibit Cabinet discussion of matters of significant public policy. The Supreme Court decided that the documents should be produced for the trial judge's inspection so that the judge, and not the executive, might decide the proper balance to be taken between the competing interests of government confidentiality and the proper administration of justice. The judge will ensure that no disclosure is made that unnecessarily interferes with confidential government communication.[45]

(f) Identity of Informers

An aspect of Crown privilege, or public interest immunity, is the long-established rule that the identity of informers should be protected from disclosure; the information is not protected from disclosure, but only its source, unless disclosure of the former would disclose the latter.[46] The public has an interest in ensuring that the lines of communication between the police and sources of information regarding the criminal activity be kept open. The privilege, born out of concerns to the administration of criminal justice, is also available now in the conduct of civil proceedings.[47]

This privilege is not absolute. If the trial judge determines that the identity of the informer is necessary to the accused's right to make full answer and defence, one public interest is in conflict with another and protection of the accused will prevail.[48] There will need to be disclosure if the informer is a material witness to the crime,[49] if the informer was the agent provocateur of the crime, or if an attack is made on the constitutionality of a search and the warrant was issued on information supplied by an informer.[50]

---

45 See also *Smerchanski v. Lewis* (1981), 58 C.C.C. (2d) 328 (Ont. C.A.).

46 *R. v. Hardy* (1794), 24 Howell's State Trials 199; *R. v. Hunter* (1987), 34 C.C.C. (3d) 14 (Ont. C.A.); and *R. v. Scott*, [1990] 3 S.C.R. 979. For recent recognition see now *R. v. Leipert* (1997), 4 C.R. (5th) 259 (S.C.C.).

47 *Canada (Solicitor General) v. Royal Commission Re Health Records, supra*, note 38; and *Bisaillon v. Keable* (1983), 7 C.C.C. (3d) 385 (S.C.C.).

48 *Marks v. Beyfus* (1890), 25 Q.B.D. 494 at 498 (C.A.); and *R. v. Scott, supra*, note 46.

49 *R. v. Davies* (1982), 1 C.C.C. (3d) 299 (Ont. C.A.).

50 *R. v. Hunter, supra*, note 46.

(g) Other Privileged Communications

Aside from the specific class privileges discussed above, there is a residual discretion in a trial judge to protect other confidential communications on a case-by-case basis. In *Slavutych*,[51] the Supreme Court recognized that a judge has the power to grant a privilege with respect to a communication if four criteria are met:

1. The communication must have originated in a confidence that it would not be disclosed.
2. The element of confidentiality must be essential to the satisfactory maintenance of the relationship between the parties.
3. The relationship must be one which the community feels ought to be fostered.
4. The injury that would inure to the relationship by disclosure must be greater than the benefit gained for the correct disposal of the litigation.

Notice the difficult balancing exercise called for in the fourth criterion.

In *Gruenke*,[52] the accused was charged with murder. There had been conversations between the accused and her pastor concerning the killing. Evidence of these had been received at trial and the accused was convicted. The Supreme Court had to decide whether these conversations were confidential communications the disclosure of which ought not to have been compelled in accordance with the principles accepted in *Slavutych*. The Court distinguished two categories of privilege: a blanket, *prima facie*, common law, or "class" privilege on the one hand, and a "case by case" privilege on the other. With the class privilege there would be a presumption of inadmissibility once it was established that the relationship fit within the class. It would be for the opposing party to persuade that the communications should not be privileged in their particular case, why their communications fitted within an exception to the general rule. The judicial creation of a class or *prima facie* privilege for religious communications would be akin to the existing class privileges for solicitor-client and marital communications. The term "case by case" privilege would apply to a situation where non-disclosure could be claimed for communications, for which there was no presumption that they were privileged, by the claimant satisfying the criteria of the Court in *Slavutych*. The majority in *Gruenke* opted for the case by case or *ad hoc* route. The majority then embarked on a case by case analysis and determined that the criteria were not met, indeed that the communica-

---

51 *Slavutych v. Baker* (1975), 55 D.L.R. (3d) 224 (S.C.C.); and *R. v. S. (R.J.)* (1985), 19 C.C.C. (3d) 115 (Ont. C.A.).
52 *R. v. Fosty*, [1991] 3 S.C.R. 263.

tions in *Gruenke* did not even satisfy the first requirement, that they originated in a confidence that they would not be disclosed.

More recently our highest Court has allowed that there might be a privilege for records kept at a sexual assault counselling centre. The Court recognized, however, the competing public interest of ensuring the accused received a fair trial. In *O'Connor*,[53] the accused was charged with a number of sexual offences. Defence counsel obtained a pre-trial order requiring that the Crown disclose the complainants' entire medical, counselling and school records and that the complainants authorize production of such records. The accused later applied for a judicial stay of proceedings based on non-disclosure of several items. Crown counsel submitted that uninhibited disclosure of medical and therapeutic records would revictimize the victims. When the Crown was unable to guarantee that full disclosure had been made the trial judge stayed the proceedings.

The majority in *O'Connor* were of the view that the Crown's disclosure obligations were unaffected by the confidential nature of therapeutic records when the records were in the possession of the Crown. When that was the case the complainants' privacy interests in the records did not need to be balanced against the right of the accused to make full answer and defence; concerns relating to privacy or privilege disappeared when the documents were in the Crown's possession.[54] The majority decided that when the defence seeks such information in the hands of a third party the onus should be on the accused to satisfy a judge that the information is likely to be relevant. In the context of disclosure, the meaning of "relevance" is whether the information may be useful to the defence. While likely relevance was the appropriate threshold for the first stage of the two-step procedure, the majority determined that it should not be interpreted as an onerous burden upon the accused. The minority saw the first stage burden on an accused as significant and, if it could not be met, the application for production should be dismissed as amounting to no more that a fishing expedition. For the minority the mere fact that the complainant had received treatment or counselling could not be presumed to be relevant to the trial. If the accused satisfies this onus, the judge should examine the records to determine whether, and to what extent, it is to be produced to the accused.

The majority said that when deciding whether to order production, the following factors were to be considered:

1. the extent to which the record was necessary for the accused to make full answer and defence;

---

53   *R. v. O'Connor* (1995), 44 C.R. (4th) 1 (S.C.C.).

54   The minority decided that the appeal did not concern the extent of the Crown's obligation to disclose private records in its possession and that any comment on such a question was strictly *obiter*.

2. the probative value of the record;
3. the nature and extent of the reasonable expectation of privacy vested in that record;
4. whether production of the record would be premised upon any discriminatory belief or bias; and
5. the potential prejudice to the complainant's dignity, privacy or security of the person.

The majority specifically rejected two other factors suggested by the minority: the extent to which production of records of this nature would frustrate society's interest in encouraging the reporting of sexual offences and the acquisition of treatment by victims as well as the effect on the integrity of the trial process of producing, or failing to produce, the record.

Following *O'Connor*, Parliament enacted legislation to restrict the production of records in sexual offence proceedings. The legislation[55] in large measure reflects the minority position in *O'Connor*. This legislation was held constitutional by the Supreme Court.[56]

3. Privilege Against Self-Incrimination

In the beginning years of trial by jury the accused in the common law courts was questioned concerning the charges against him. It seemed the sensible thing to do. Gradually however, during the seventeenth century, as a reaction, or perhaps an overreaction, towards the inquisitorial methods of the Ecclesiastical Courts and the Court of Star Chamber, accused persons in the common law courts began to resist such questioning and by 1700 it was recognized that no person, in any court, whether he be an accused or merely a witness, could be compelled to answer if the answer would tend to incriminate. The common law privilege against self-incrimination was born.

Until the end of the nineteenth century the accused was not able to give testimony on oath for two reasons. First, he was regarded as incompetent because of his obvious interest in the outcome of the proceedings. Second, it was regarded as a violation of his privilege against self-incrimination to place him on the horns of a dilemma: should he choose to testify falsely gaining temporal relief but everlasting damnation or testify truthfully and forfeit his liberty? Perhaps a trilemma in that should he choose not to testify, and it being known that he was able, he risked an inference of guilt being drawn from his silence. By the end of the nineteenth century statutory

---

55 See ss 278.1 to 278.9 of the Criminal Code.
56 See *R. v. Mills* (1999) 28 C.R. (5th) 207 (S.C.C.). For the proper procedure in a civil case where production is sought see *M.(A.) v. Ryan* (1997) 4 C.R. (5th) 220 (S.C.C.).

reforms made the accused competent for the defence. The common law position of non-compellability at the instance of the prosecution remained. Section 4 of the *Canada Evidence Act* provides:

> (1) Every person charged with an offence, and, except as otherwise provided in this section, the wife or husband, as the case may be, of the person so charged, is a competent witness for the defence, whether the person so charged is charged solely or jointly with any other person.

The Charter similarly provides: "11 (c) [any person charged with an offence has the right] not to be compelled to be a witness in proceedings against that person in respect of the offence."[57]

It is important to recognize that this privilege, in its origins and as later interpreted in Canada[58] operated to protect a person from being compelled to give evidence before a court or like tribunal. It was also restricted to testimonial evidence. Taking bodily samples, fingerprints or photographs were not seen as captured by the privilege.[59] In short, the privilege in Canada was seen to be reflected simply, and solely, in the accused's non-compellability at trial. The accused, pursuant to the legislation, was a competent witness for the defence. It was up to the accused to decide whether he would go into the box.

In Canada, the legislation also provided that no witness, including the accused who chose to become a witness, could refuse to answer a question on the grounds that the answer might tend to criminate. Rather, the legislation provided that he was obliged to answer but the answer could not be used against him in later proceedings. For example, the *Canada Evidence Act* provides:

> 5. (1) No witness shall be excused from answering any question on the ground that the answer to the question may tend to criminate him, or may tend to establish his liability to a civil proceeding at the instance of the Crown or of any person.
>
> (2) Where with respect to any question a witness objects to answer on the ground that his answer may tend to criminate him, or may tend to establish his liability to a civil proceeding at the instance of the Crown or of any person, and if but for this Act, or the Act of any provincial legislature, the witness would therefore have been excused from answering the question, then although the witness is by reason of this Act or the provincial Act compelled to answer, the answer so given shall not be used or admissible in evidence against him in any criminal trial or other criminal proceeding against him thereafter taking

---

57 *Constitution Act*, 1982, R.S.C. 1985, App. II, No. 44.

58 *R. v. Curr* (1972), 7 C.C.C. (2d) 181 (S.C.C.), interpreting the privilege as bestowed by the *Canadian Bill of Rights*.

59 *R. v. Marcoux* (1975), 24 C.C.C. (2d) 1 (S.C.C.).

place, other than a prosecution for perjury in the giving of that evidence or for the giving of contradictory evidence.

Similar provisions exist in provincial legislation.[60]

The Charter similarly provides:

13 A witness who testifies in any proceedings has the right not to have any incriminating evidence so given used to incriminate that witness in any other proceeding, except in a prosecution for perjury or for the giving of contradictory evidence.

Notice that the Charter protection is automatic and does not depend on the witness's objection. Notice that the prohibition against subsequent use is limited to foreclose use of the statement; it does not foreclose use of evidence derived from the statement. For example, suppose a witness is called to testify at a coroner's inquest. He is asked questions concerning his consumption of alcohol on the evening of the fatal automobile accident. He objects to answer on the grounds that the answer might incriminate. The coroner notes his objection and, following the legislation,[61] advises the witness that he needs to answer the question. The witness testifies that he had six beers at Joe's Bar on the evening in question. Should the witness later be prosecuted for manslaughter for the death arising out of the accident the Crown cannot lead evidence of the witness's earlier sworn statement. But, and it's a big but, the Crown could lead evidence from Joe that the accused had six beers at his place on the evening in question.

(a) Inferences from the Accused's Silence At Trial

When the accused was made a competent witness at the end of the nineteenth century, the change brought problems for the accused. He then faced the dilemma of choosing between not going into the stand, with the trier perhaps inferring guilt from his silence, or exposing himself to the oath and cross-examination.

In *R. v. Noble*[62] the manager of an apartment building found two young men in the parking area of his building, one of whom appeared to be

---

60 For similar provincial and territorial provisions, see: R.S.A. 1980, c. A-21, s. 6; R.S.B.C. 1996, c. 124, s. 4; R.S.M. 1987, c. E.150, s. 6; R.S.N.B. 1973, c. E-11, s. 6; R.S.N. 1970, c. 115, s. 3A; R.S.N.W.T. 1998, c. E-8, s. 7; R.S.N.S. 1989, c. 154, s. 59; R.S.O. 1990, c. E.23, s. 9; R.S.P.E.I. 1988, c. E-11, s. 6; R.S.S. 1978, c. S-16, s. 37; and R.S.Y. 1986, c. 57, s. 7.

61 The inquest would be governed by provincial legislation but it has legislation parallelling s. 5: see *supra*, note 60. The protection flows from the applicable legislation. Testimony compelled at a civil hearing by provincial legislation would be protected against subsequent use in a criminal case by the, there applicable, federal legislation.

62 (1997) 6 C.R. (5th) 1 (S.C.C.).

attempting to break into a car with a screwdriver. When the manager asked the man for identification, he handed over an expired driver's licence. The manager testified that he thought the photograph on the licence accurately depicted the man in front of him in the garage and told the man that he could retrieve the licence from the police. The accused was eventually charged with breaking and entering and having in his possession an instrument suitable for the purpose of breaking into a motor vehicle. At trial, neither the manager nor anyone else could identify the accused, but the trial judge concluded that he as the trier of fact could compare the picture in the driver's licence with the accused in the courtroom and conclude that the driver's licence accurately depicted the accused. He also was satisfied that the building manager would have carefully examined the licence at the time of the incident. The trial judge noted that the accused faced an overwhelming case to meet as a result of the licence, yet remained silent. In the trial judge's view, he could draw "almost an adverse inference" that "certainly may add to the weight of the Crown's case on the issue of identification". The accused was convicted on both counts. The Court of Appeal set aside the convictions and ordered a new trial. A 5:4 majority of the Supreme Court dismissed the Crown's appeal. For the majority the use of the accused's silence to help establish guilt beyond a reasonable doubt was contrary to the rationale behind the right to silence. The minority pointed to a number of the Court's previous judgments that seemed to indicate that the use of the accused's silence at trial was permissible.[63]

(b) Comments on the Accused's Failure to Testify

The *Canada Evidence Act* provides:

> 4(6). The failure of the person charged, or the wife or husband of that person, to testify shall not be made the subject of comment by the judge or by counsel for the prosecution.

The first thing to notice about the Canadian provision is that our courts have decided that the comment is only prohibited in cases of trial by jury and when the comment is made in the presence of the jury.[64] Perhaps such reasoning was born of a belief that in trials by judge alone the accused's failure to testify would not be magnified out of its proper proportion, since a trial judge is able to place it in its proper perspective. The next thing to

---

63 For comments on *Noble* see Delisle and Stuart at (1997), 6 C.R. (5th) 5 and 8. See also, Delisle, *Silence at Trial: Inferences and Comments*, (1997) 1 C.R. (5th) 313.

64 *R. v. Binder* (1948), 92 C.C.C. 20 (Ont. C.A.), followed in *Pratte v. Maher*, [1965] 1 C.C.C. 77 (Que. C.A.), *R. v. Bouchard*, [1970] 5 C.C.C. 95 (N.B. C.A.), *Ontario (Attorney General) v. Clark*, 1967 1 C.C.C. 131 (Ont. H.C.), affirmed [1967] 2 C.C.C. 196n (C.A.).

notice is that comment by an accused on his own or his co-accused's failure to take the stand is not foreclosed by the section.[65]

The next thing to notice about s. 4(6) is that there are comments and then there are *comments*. Sometimes, what appears to be a comment is interpreted to be rather a statement and not prohibited. In *Avon*,[66] the trial judge said to the jury:

> The accused did not testify. Evidently, he could have done so. He is not obliged to do so. I must tell you immediately . . .. it is not because the accused did not testify that you should believe that he could be guilty . . .. Actually you have merely the Crown's evidence. The defense did not call witnesses, and the accused did not testify: he did not have to. It is up to the Crown to prove its case.[67]

The Supreme Court said this was a "statement" of an accused's right not to testify, rather than a "comment" on his failure to do so and could not be construed as prejudicial to the accused or such to suggest to the jurors that his silence was used to cloak his guilt.

In *McConnell*,[68] the accused were charged with possession of house-breaking instruments. They had offered an explanation to the police at the time but they did not testify. The trial judge told the jury:

> You are not to be influenced in your decision by either of the accused not going into the witness box and testifying, but the Court does point out that these explanations . . . when made were not made under oath and it is not only for that reason alone, but for any other number of reasons that may occur to you, to decide if you will accept these explanations.[69]

The accused's appeals were dismissed as the Court noted that the language used by the trial judge was not so much a "comment" on the failure of the persons charged to testify as a "statement" of their right to refrain from doing so, and a trial judge is not precluded from explaining to juries the law with respect to the rights of accused persons in this regard.[70]

In *Noble*,[71] Lamer, C.J. in dissent, suggested that according to the majority s. 4 (6) was unconstitutional. He reasoned that if the jury was not entitled to draw any inference from the accused's failure to testify it should

---

65 See *R. v. Creighton*, [1995] 1 S.C.R. 858.

66 *Avon v. R.* (1971), 21 D.L.R. (3d) 442 (S.C.C.).

67 *Ibid.* at 455.

68 *R. v. McConnell*, [1968] 4 C.C.C. 257 (S.C.C.).

69 *Ibid.* at 260.

70 For a list of cases setting out what comments are within the section and what are without, see McWilliams, *Canadian Criminal Evidence*, 3d ed. (Aurora, Ont.: Canada Law Book, 1990), 30:10500.

71 *R. v. Noble* (1996), 47 C.R. (4th) 258 (B.C. C.A.), affirmed [1997] 1 S.C.R. 874.

be told just that by the judge and yet the section foreclosed that advice. The majority said the issue was not before it.

(c) The Creation of a Right to Silence in Canada

By statute and the Charter the accused is not a compellable witness. If the accused chooses to testify at trial he thereby becomes a witness and the statute provides that he is not entitled to refuse to answer questions which might tend to criminate.[72] The statute and the Charter appear to be very specific as to the scope of a person's privilege against self-incrimination. It bestows non-compellability only on those who are charged with an offence and that protection is only in proceedings in respect to that offence. It grants subsequent use immunity to those who are asked questions which tend to incriminate but the immunity is against the use of the evidence given; there is no immunity against the use of evidence discovered or derived from the answers. It is noteworthy as well that while many rights are bestowed in the Charter, from the right to counsel to the right to be secure against unreasonable search and seizure, there is nothing in the Charter that speaks to a right to silence. However, there is in the Charter a broad and mysterious section:

> 7. Everyone has the right to life, liberty and security of the person and the right not to be deprived thereof except in accordance with the principles of fundamental justice.

In *Hebert*,[73] the parties agreed that s. 7 accorded a right to silence to a detained person but disagreed over the extent of the right. The Court accepted the parties' concession and occupied itself with articulating its views on the scope of the right. In that case it was decided that a detained person's pre-trial right to silence was violated when an undercover officer elicited a confession from the accused in his jail cell. The Court decided that the admissibility of confessions rested not just on considerations of trustworthiness but also on the privilege against self-incrimination and decided the confession had to be excluded.[74]

(d) A Principle Versus a Privilege

Until quite recently there was not in Canada a broad principle against self-incrimination.[75] There existed two protections: non-compellability at

---

72 *Supra*, this Chapter, Privilege Against Self-Incrimination.
73 *R. v. Hebert* (1990), 77 C.R. (3d) 145 (S.C.C.).
74 Just before the Charter came into being, the Court had concluded the opposite: see *R. v. Rothman* (1981), 59 C.C.C. (2d) 30 (S.C.C.).
75 See, *e.g.*, Ratushny, "Is There a Right Against Self-Incrimination in Canada?" (1973) 19 McGill L.J. 1, and Iacobucci J. in *R. v. S. (R.J.)* (1995), 36 C.R. (4th) 1 (S.C.C.).

trial,[76] and protection against subsequent use of evidence given at a prior proceeding.[77] The right of a suspect not to say anything to the police was not the result of some general right of no self-incrimination, but was merely the exercise by him of the general right enjoyed in this country by anyone to do whatever one pleases, saying what one pleases or choosing not to say certain things, unless obliged to do otherwise by law.[78]

In *Dubois*,[79] the Court addressed the admissibility into evidence of statements made by an accused at his first trial for murder into the second trial. The Court decided that this was a violation of s.13 of the Charter. In doing so, the Court noted that otherwise the Crown would be able to do indirectly what it couldn't do directly; by virtue of s.11(c) of the Charter, the Crown could not compel the accused to testify. It also was observed that permitting receipt of his earlier testimony would permit an indirect violation of the right to be presumed innocent as guaranteed by s. 11 (d) of the Charter. The Court found underlying the Charter rights in ss. 11(c), (d) and 13, and the benefit of an initial right to silence at trial, the common concept of a "case to meet".[80]

In *P. (M.B.)*,[81] the Court, deciding it was wrong to permit the prosecution to re-open its case after the accused had outlined its defence, repeated the thought of a "case to meet", and spoke of the broad protection afforded to accused persons, which the Court said was best described in terms of the overarching *principle* against self-incrimination.[82] This principle, according to the Court, was firmly rooted in the common law and was a fundamental principle of justice under s. 7 of the Charter. The Court recognized that apart from the *privilege* against self-incrimination, which grants the specific protections outlined above, there is also a *principle* against self-incrimination which may give greater protection than formerly contemplated.

In *Jones*,[83] Chief Justice Lamer expanded on what he had earlier written about the principle. He said that any state action that coerced an individual to furnish evidence against himself in a proceeding in which the individual

---

76 Section 4 of the *Canada Evidence Act* and s. 11(c) of the Charter.

77 Section 5(2) of the *Canada Evidence Act* and s. 13 of the Charter.

78 *Per* Lamer J. in *R. v. Rothman, supra,* note 74.

79 *R. v. Dubois*, [1985] 2 S.C.R. 350.

80 This concept was taken from the analysis of Ratushny, "The Role of the Accused at the Trial Stage", in Tarnopolsky & Beaudoin (eds.), *The Canadian Charter of Rights and Freedoms* (1982) at 358-359.

81 *Supra,* note 60.

82 *Ibid.* at 226.

83 *R. v. Jones* (1994), 30 C.R. (4th) 1 at 41 (S.C.C.). Although speaking in dissent, the Chief Justice's remarks regarding the principle seem to have been adopted by, at least, most of the Court. In *R. v. S. (R.J.), supra,* note 75, Iacobucci J., for himself and three others, decided that the dissent was only on the question of whether dangerous offender proceedings serve to incriminate further a person who has already been convicted.

and the state were adversaries violated the *principle* against self-incrimination. He described the *privilege* as the narrow traditional common law rule relating only to testimonial evidence at trial.

(e) New Charter Protections for Potential Accused

There has been, in the past, an ability in the state to avoid the strictures of the privilege against self-incrimination, by compelling a suspect or an accused to testify at some other proceeding prior to his criminal trial thereby discovering evidence usable against him at his trial.[84] The court may have now moved to foreclose that possibility.

The accused in *S. (R.J.)*[85] was charged with break, enter and theft. M. was charged separately with the same offence. The charges were laid separately because of a procedure at Youth Court which called for different trials dependent on the age of the youths. M. was subpoenaed by the Crown as its main witness at the accused's trial. The subpoena was quashed on the basis that otherwise M.'s right to silence under s. 7 would be violated. *S. (R.J.)* involved a complex series of divided opinions in the Supreme Court. A few months later, in *Branch*,[86] the Court amplified its earlier thoughts on compellability. The Supreme Court decided that the principle against self-incrimination required that persons who were compelled to testify might need to be provided with subsequent derivative-use immunity in addition to the use immunity guaranteed by s. 13 of the Charter. The accused would have the evidentiary burden of showing a plausible connection between the compelled testimony and the evidence later sought to be adduced. Once this was done, in order to have the evidence admitted, the Crown would have to satisfy the court on a balance of probabilities that the authorities would have discovered the impugned derivative evidence absent the compelled testimony. They also decided that in addition courts can, in certain circumstances, grant exemptions from compulsion to testify. The crucial question was whether the predominant purpose for seeking the evidence was to obtain incriminating evidence against the person compelled to testify or rather some legitimate public purpose. That test was seen to strike the appropriate balance between the interests of the state in obtaining the evidence for a valid public purpose on the one hand, and the right to silence of the person compelled to testify on the other.[87]

---

84 See generally, Ratushny, *Self-Incrimination in the Canadian Criminal Process* (Toronto: Carswell, 1979) at 347-402.

85 *R. v. S. (R.J.)*, *supra*, note 75.

86 *British Columbia (Securities Commission) v. Branch* (1995), 38 C.R. (4th) 133 (S.C.C.).

87 See also *R. v. Jobin* (1995), 38 C.R. (4th) 176 (S.C.C.); and *R. v. Primeau* (1995), 38 C.R. (4th) 189 (S.C.C.).

4. Confessions

Pre-trial statements of an accused are admissions and therefore qualify as an exception to the hearsay rule and are receivable for their truth. The courts, however, concerned as to the possibility of false statements, erected an additional hurdle to their reception. A statement by an accused, a confession, was admissible at common law only if the prosecution established beyond a reasonable doubt that the statement was voluntary in the sense that it was not obtained as the result of promise of favour or fear of prejudice held out by a person in authority.[88] In later decisions, the court decided that an involuntary confession could be excluded, though there had been no offer of favour or prejudice if, considering all the circumstances, the statement was not voluntary in the ordinary English sense of the word. For example, a statement by a person shortly after a motor vehicle accident, when the person was still in a state of shock, could be excluded as involuntary if there was a reasonable doubt that the words were the product of an operating mind.[89]

For some time the confession rule was thought to be applicable only to inculpatory statements. Only when the prosecution was tendering the statement for its truth, inculpating the accused in the crime, need the prosecution prove voluntariness. In *Piche*,[90] the accused was charged with murder. She told the police that she'd had an argument with the deceased that evening, she'd left the apartment and he was then sleeping. At the trial she told quite a different story. She admitted the shooting but said it had been accidental. The Supreme Court decided that, whether inculpatory or exculpatory, statements to the police needed to be proved voluntary.

The voluntariness of a statement is determined on a *voir dire* in the absence of the jury. The accused may concede voluntariness and waive the requirement but this needs to be express. Even if there is waiver the trial judge might decide that a *voir dire* be held.[91] It is for the trial judge to decide whether the statement was voluntary. If that preliminary condition of admissibility is satisfied the evidence is given to the jury. There may be contradictory evidence as to what, if anything, was in fact said. In such a case the normal rules apply and it is for the jury to decide, what, if anything,

---

88 The test was articulated in *Ibrahim v. R.*, [1914] A.C. 599 (Hong Kong P.C.) and accepted in Canada in *R. v. Prosko* (1922), 63 S.C.R. 226 and *R. v. Boudreau* (1949), 7 C.R. 427 (S.C.C.).

89 *R. v. Ward* (1979), 44 C.C.C. (2d) 498 (S.C.C.). To similar effect, see *R. v. Horvath* (1979), 44 C.C.C. (2d) 385 (S.C.C.) and *R. v. Nagotcha* (1980), 51 C.C.C. (2d) 353 (S.C.C.). With respect to the onus of proof, see *R. v. Lapointe* (1983), 9 C.C.C. (3d) 366 at 383 (Ont. C.A.), affirmed (1987), 35 C.C.C. (3d) 287 (S.C.C.).

90 *R. v. Piche*, [1971] S.C.R. 23.

91 See *R. v. Park* (1981), 59 C.C.C. (2d) 385 (S.C.C.).

was actually said.[92] Once the judge has determined that the statement ought to be received much of the same evidence heard on the *voir dire* will be repeated for the jury's benefit so that the jury can decide what weight to give to it. If the trial is by judge sitting alone it is somewhat common practice, to save time, for the parties to agree that the evidence taken on the *voir dire* be taken as if it was given at the trial proper.

Periodically, some courts would state that an accused's involuntary confession was rejected not just out of concern for its trustworthiness but also because of the privilege against self-incrimination.[93] This position was rejected by our highest Court. In *Wray*,[94] the accused had been charged with murder. He had given a statement to the police in circumstances which were found to be coercive. The trial judge rejected the statement. The Crown then offered evidence that as a result of the accused's statement they were able to find the murder weapon. The Crown took the position that the portion of the accused's statement that was confirmed as true by the finding of the gun should be received as truth was the only concern of the confession rule. The trial judge excluded the offered evidence and the accused was acquitted. The Court of Appeal agreed with the trial judge that there was a power in a trial judge to reject even highly probative evidence if reception of the same would bring the administration of justice into disrepute. The Supreme Court rejected such a notion. The Court decided that there was only one purpose underlying the confession rule and that was concern as to trustworthiness. At common law there was no power in a trial judge to exclude evidence of substantial probative value.

The *Canadian Charter of Rights and Freedoms* provides, as a remedy for any violation of a Charter right:

> 24(2) Where, in proceedings under subsection (1), a court concludes that evidence was obtained in a manner that infringed or denied any rights or freedoms guaranteed by this Charter, the evidence shall be excluded if it is established that, having regard to all the circumstances, the admission of it in the proceedings would bring the administration of justice into disrepute.

Section 10(b) of the Charter provides that everyone has the right on arrest or detention "to retain and instruct counsel without delay and to be informed of that right."

In *Clarkson*,[95] the accused was very intoxicated when she was charged with the murder of her husband. She was given the customary warning and informed as to her right to counsel. She said there was no point in having

---

92   *Ibid.*

93   See, *e.g., Commissioners of Customs & Excise v. Harz* (1966), [1967] 1 A.C. 760 at 820 (H.L.) and *R. v. Rothman, supra,* note 74, *per* Lamer and Estey JJ.

94   *R. v. Wray* (1970), 11 D.L.R. (3d) 673 (S.C.C.).

95   *R. v. Clarkson* (1986), 50 C.R. (3d) 289 (S.C.C.).

counsel and she underwent police questioning while still drunk and quite emotional. The trial judge excluded her statements, applying the common law confession rule, and deciding that the accused did not appreciate the consequences of making the statements. She was acquitted. On appeal, the Court said the trial judge had erred in focussing on the accused's appreciation of the consequences and that the proper test was whether an accused was in a sufficiently functional state to give probative value to her words. On further appeal, the Supreme Court recognized that there was authority for both viewpoints but decided that it was not necessary to resolve the issue as the case could be decided on the basis of the violation of the accused's Charter right to counsel.[96] The Court decided that the accused's statements were properly excluded because the accused's right to counsel had been violated because there had been no effective waiver of that right as the accused did not appreciate the consequences of her waiver.

Section 7 of the Charter provides:

> Everyone has the right to life, liberty and security of the person and the right not to be deprived thereof except in accordance with principles of fundamental justice.

In *Hebert*,[97] the Court decided that there was, within s. 7 of the Charter, a right to remain silent and any statement obtained in violation of that right could be excluded under s. 24(2). In *Hebert*, an inculpatory statement was obtained from an accused by an undercover officer lodged in the accused's cell. The officer had engaged the accused in conversation despite the fact that the accused had earlier indicated to the police that he did not want to say anything to them about the matter. Such a statement would not have been excluded under the common law confession rule since the accused did not know that he was speaking to a person in authority,[98] but the Court decided the trial judge was right to exclude it under the Charter. In finding the statement to have been taken in violation of principles of fundamental justice, the Court reviewed the common law, noted the controversy whether one or two reasons for the confession rule existed, and seemed to decide that confessions at common law should be excluded not just out of concern for trustworthiness but also because of the privilege against self-incrimination. Remember, at common law there is an obligation on the Crown to prove a statement voluntary beyond a reasonable doubt. The onus is on the prosecution. Under the Charter the accused has the onus of establishing a

---

96   In *R. v. Whittle* (1994), 32 C.R. (4th) 1 (S.C.C.), the Court seems to have decided that the view of the Court of Appeal regarding the common law was the correct point of view. For criticism see Delisle, "*Whittle* and *Tran:* Conflicting Messages on How Much an Accused Must Understand" (1994), 32 C.R. (4th) 29.

97   *R. v. Hebert, supra,* note 73.

98   *R. v. Rothman, supra,* note 74.

violation of his Charter rights and also has the onus of establishing that the statement ought to be excluded.[99]

The Court has recently reviewed in a most comprehensive way the common law confession rule. In *R. v. Oickle*[100] the Court emphasized that while reliability was one concern underlying the confession rule the inquiry into voluntariness was a broad inquiry as it is also concerned with maintaining the integrity of the criminal justice system. The Court identified four categories triggering the confession rule: threats or promises, operating mind, oppression and police trickery. The last category required that the trick be such as would shock the conscience of the community.[101]

5. Exclusion of Improperly Obtained Evidence

We've seen that at common law there was no power in a trial judge to exclude evidence based on how the evidence was obtained. If the evidence had probative value the court was, aside from confessions, not concerned with how the evidence was obtained.[102] If real evidence — the gun, the narcotics — was obtained by illegal methods, Canadian courts said the remedy for such illegality was not to be found in excluding the evidence in the subsequent prosecution of the accused. The aggrieved could seek a remedy in the civil courts or lay a complaint with the appropriate police governing body.

Section 24(2) gave a discretion to the trial judge to exclude if the evidence was obtained in violation of the accused's rights. As with any discretion in the law of evidence the appropriate factors for consideration were spelled out. In *Collins*,[103] our highest court articulated those factors:

1. What kind of evidence was obtained?
2. What Charter right was infringed?
3. Was the Charter violation serious or was it of a merely technical nature?
4. Was it deliberate, wilful, flagrant, or inadvertent, committed in good faith?
5. Did it occur in circumstances of urgency or necessity?

---

99 For discussion of the relationship between the common law confession rule and the right to silence protection under the Charter, see P. Healy, "The Value of Silence" (1990), 74 C.R. (3d) 176; P. Healy, "The Right to Remain Silent: Value Added, But How Much?" (1990), 77 C.R. (3d) 199; and D.M. Tanovich, "The Charter Right to Silence and the Unchartered Waters of a New Voluntary Confession Rule" (1992), 9 C.R. (4th) 24.

100 (2001), 36 C.R. (5th) 129 (S.C.C.)

101 For a critical comment see Stuart, *Oickle: The Supreme Court's Recipe for Coercive Interrogation*, (2001) 36 C.R. (5th) 188.

102 *R. v. Wray, supra*, note 94.

103 *R. v. Collins* (1987), 56 C.R. (3d) 193 (S.C.C.).

6. Were there other investigatory techniques available?
7. Would the evidence have been obtained in any event?
8. Is the offence serious?
9. Is the evidence essential to substantiate the charge?

The Court went on to note that it was useful to group the factors. Factors 1 and 2 were seen to affect the fairness of the trial. For example, if the evidence was a statement, taken in violation of the accused's right to counsel, guaranteed by s. 10(b) of the Charter, the accused was conscripted against his own interests and a court should more readily exclude such as receiving the same would impact negatively on the fairness of the trial. Factors 3 to 7 were regarded as impacting on the seriousness of the violation and thus to the disrepute that would result from judicial acceptance of evidence obtained through that violation. Factors 8 and 9 were factors that related to the effect of excluding the evidence. The Court recognized that, particularly if the offence was serious and the evidence was necessary to its successful prosecution, exclusion of the evidence would bring the administration of justice into disrepute.

In *Manninen*,[104] the accused was charged with robbery. After his arrest the police asked him questions regarding his involvement. The accused said he didn't want to say anything until he'd seen his lawyer. The police then asked him where the knife was that he'd used in the robbery. The accused said he'd only had the gun in the store and the knife was in the tool box in the car. The Court decided the accused's right to counsel had been violated as the police should have ceased all questioning when the accused said he wanted to see his lawyer until the accused had a reasonable opportunity to consult with counsel. The Court noted that the evidence obtained was self-incriminatory and the use of the same following the denial of the accused's right to counsel would affect the fairness of the trial and thus will generally bring the administration of justice into disrepute and need to be excluded.

If, on the other hand, the evidence was real in nature, *e.g.*, narcotics, discovered as the result of a violation of the accused's right to be secure against unreasonable search and seizure, guaranteed by s. 8 of the Charter, receiving the evidence would not affect the fairness of the trial as the evidence existed apart from the violation. In *Black*,[105] the accused was charged with attempted murder. Her right to counsel was breached and the Court decided that the incriminating statements obtained from her would have to be excluded as receiving them would affect the fairness of the trial. The Court excluded evidence of her involvement in the finding of the knife. For real evidence to be excluded the Court needed to consider factors 3 to

---

104 *R. v. Manninen* (1987), 58 C.R. (3d) 97 (S.C.C.).
105 *R. v. Black* (1989), 50 C.C.C. (3d) 1 (S.C.C.).

7. The Charter violation would have to be quite serious and the court would be interested in whether the evidence would have been discovered in any event. The Court in *Black* noted that the knife itself was real evidence which existed whether or not there had been a breach, it did not come into existence as the result of the accused's participation and the police would have no doubt found it with or without her assistance. Therefore, the Court concluded the administration of justice would not be brought into disrepute by the admission of the real evidence.

Later decisions modified the *Collins* test. It has since been decided that if, on considering the first group of factors, the judge is satisfied that receipt of the evidence would render the trial unfair there may be no need to go on to consider the second group. The first two groups are seen to be alternate grounds for exclusion. If, for example, the trial judge decided that the evidence would make the trial unfair he would not decide to receive it on the basis that the violation was made in good faith.[106] Sometimes, however, all the factors continue to be considered.[107]

The Court further modified the *Collins* test in *R. v. Stillman*.[108] The Court decided that as a first step in the trial fairness analysis it was necessary to classify the type of evidence gained; conscriptive or non-conscriptive. Admission of evidence which fell into the non-conscriptive category would, per *Collins*, rarely operate to render the trial unfair. If the evidence was classified as non-conscriptive the court was to move on to consider the second and third *Collins* factors. Conscriptive evidence would generally be excluded without considering the second and third factors. However, if the conscriptive evidence would have been discovered by in any event by non-conscriptive means reception would not render the trial unfair. For the court conscriptive evidence would include compelled self-incriminating statements, compelled provision of bodily substances and compelled use of the body.[109]

---

106 *R. v. Hebert, supra,* note 73, *per* Sopinka J., adopted in *R. v. Mellenthin* (1992), 16 C.R. (4th) 273 (S.C.C.); *R. v. Elshaw* (1991), 7 C.R. (4th) 333 (S.C.C.); *R. v. Broyles* (1991), 9 C.R. (4th) 1 (S.C.C.); and *R. v. Burlingham* (1995), 38 C.R. (4th) 265 (S.C.C.).

107 See, *e.g.*, *R. v. Burlingham, ibid.*

108 (1997), 5 C.R. (5th) 1 (S.C.C.).

109 See Stuart, *Stillman: Limiting Search Incident to Arrest, Consent Searches and Refining the Section* 24 (2) *Test*, (1997) 5 C.R. (5th) 99.

Index

[All references are to page numbers of the text]